CARROLL & GRAF

The Amateur Emigrant

The Amateur Emigrant

ROBERT LOUIS STEVENSON

With a Preface by
MRS. FANNY STEVENSON

CARROLL & GRAF PUBLISHERS
NEW YORK

THE AMATEUR EMIGRANT

Carroll & Graf Publishers
An Imprint of Avalon Publishing Group Incorporated
161 William Street, 16th Floor
New York, NY 10038

Copyright © 1896 by Robert Louis Stevenson

First Carroll & Graf trade paperback edition 2002

Library of Congress Cataloging-in-Publication Data is available.

ISBN: 0-7867-0984-7

Printed in the United States of America
Distributed by Publishers Group West

PREFACE

ONE of the closest friends of my husband's youth was a clever young man whose life, up to that time, had been mostly spent in hospitals. Embittered by poverty and suffering, his turbulent spirit revolted against law and society, and he had become an ardent socialist. I remember meeting, in his house, a party of Russian anarchists, Stepniak among them, who greeted him as "brother," shouting and laughing like schoolboys on a holiday, and declaring that if they could only meet my husband face to face they would soon make a convert of him. Indeed, up to a certain point, he sympathized with the socialists. He could not think of the innocent victims of civilization—the men who only asked for work, and could get none, while their children were starving —without raging against the existing order of things; while his own comfortable circumstances filled him with shame when he contemplated the hardships of those less fortunate than himself. But, unlike his friend, he could suggest no remedy; the assassination of individuals and bomb-throwing seeming to him not only barbaric, but silly and futile.

While he could see no royal road for others, the path for himself showed plainly enough before him, and it was his duty to swerve neither to the right nor the left. He believed he had no rights, only undeserved indulgences.

He must not eat unearned bread, but must pay the world, in some fashion, for what it gave him,—first, materially, then in kindness, sympathy, and love. Class distinctions, so strictly observed in England, he could not tolerate and never gave the slightest heed to their limitations. "Ladies?" he said in reply to an observation by a visitor, "one of the truest ladies in Bournemouth, Mrs. Waats, is at this moment washing my study windows." Once, coming upon a crowd of young roughs who were tormenting a wretched drunken creature of the streets, he pushed his way through them, and amid their jeers offered his arm to the woman and escorted her to the place she called home. "Don Quixote," he once said to my son, with a startled look, "why, *I* am Don Quixote!" Too much ease frightened him; he would occasionally insist on some sharp discomfort, such as sleeping on a mat on the floor, or dining on a ship's biscuit, to awaken him, as he said, to realities; and nothing pleased him more than to risk his life or health to serve another. Yet he never succeeded in wholly subduing the "old Adam" within him. Meanness or falsity or cruelty set his eyes blazing, and his language on such occasions became far from parliamentary.

Naturally his first visit to America, a land without class distinctions, was to him an event of extraordinary interest. The privations he endured as an amateur emigrant caused him much less suffering than his friends, who could not imagine themselves in a similar position, supposed. It was not the first time he had associated with the working-man on terms of equality; nor did it occur to him that it was a condescension on his part to join with his fellow-passengers in their attempts to make the time pass

pleasantly, or to do for them what little kindly offices came
in his way. One thing he did resent with bitterness—the
visits of the first-class passengers, who came out of curiosity into the steerage, looking about as though they were
passing through a menagerie. He never forgave "your wife,
my good man?" "Why," he would ask, "should I be her
good man any more than she my good woman? Her
question, and manner of putting it, made me understand
a great many things."

I remember, when we were living in Hyères, his receiving a letter from England that enclosed a petition asking
for the release of a noted anarchist who was said to be
dying in a French prison. This man, said the letter, had
thrown everything away for the "cause,"—his entire
fortune, his title, and his birthright as a subject of Russia,
to which he could never return; while comparatively young
in years, he presented the appearance of an old man, with
hair prematurely white and his health broken by confine-
ment in a damp, unsanitary prison. My husband's name
was to head the list. "Poor devil," he said, as he dipped his
pen in the ink. But he laid it down again thoughtfully,
and, instead of signing the petition, wrote a letter stating
that he had read the trial, and asking why the Russian gentleman had refused to say whether he had had a hand in
the blowing up of a workingman's café in Lyons, in which
catastrophe many persons, mostly peasants with their families, had been killed or shockingly injured. He could not,
he said, withhold his admiration for a man who had given
so much, but he could and would withhold his signature
until he was satisfied on this point. No such assurance
being forthcoming, the petition was returned with the

remark "I think Monsieur—had better complete his sacri-
fice by dying in prison."

For street musicians and wandering performers—
acrobats, jugglers, etc.—my husband showed an understanding and sympathy that always won their confidence.
"We're in the same boat," he would say, "earning our bread
by amusing the public." "I always divide with a brother
artist," he would remark, as he emptied his pockets into
their hands. His acquaintance with such people, and his
knowledge of the lives they led, gave him an almost mor-
bid sense of the pitiless cruelty of modern civilization. It
was only his strong intelligence and common sense that
kept him from the ranks of the anarchists. He came to
America with exaggerated views of the meaning of democ-
racy, believing that there he would find the ideal social as
well as political life. In the beginning he encountered
many rude shocks, but he soon readjusted his point of
view, though he never ceased regretting that this great
country should have been lost to England. The name of
George the Third was hardly to be spoken in his presence.
"Had it not been for that idiot," he would cry, "we should
now be one nation." Of New York, at this time, he saw
very little, but on a later visit grew to love it as he would
not have thought possible when he first arrived in America. A particularly attractive spot to him was Washington
Square, where he spent many hours sitting on the benches
under the trees enjoying the frank conversation of the
children who used the park as a playground. On one
memorable occasion he passed an afternoon there with
Mark Twain.

At first the apparent rudeness of the average American

repelled him, but when he found that the gentlest, most
kindly acts accompanied the off-hand address, his heart
warmed towards his "younger brother." In San Francisco
he made many friendships that were only broken by
death,—Mr. and Mrs. Virgil Williams, to whom he dedi-
cated *The Silverado Squatters:* Dr. Chismore, Dr. Willy,
Judge Rearden, who recognized a kindred spirit in the
unknown, shabbily dressed young Scot living in the poor
little lodging house on Bush Street kept by Mr. and Mrs.
Carson. For the last few years on each thirteenth of
November a small band of those who love to do honour to
my husband's memory have met in San Francisco to cele-
brate his birthday. Nor would the party be considered
complete without Jules Simoneau, now far past eighty
years of age, but still as clear in mind and as strong in
heart as when my husband first knew him in Monterey, the
best beloved of all the friends of that time of adversity.

The journey by emigrant train across the continent was
an experience far worse than that on shipboard, but
through all the fatigue and active misery of it my husband
managed to keep his diary posted up to date, and two
months later, in Monterey, he wrote to Mr. Colvin: *"The
Amateur Emigrant* is about half drafted. It was from
Monterey that he also wrote to Mr. Colvin: "I am a
reporter for the *Monterey Californian* at a salary of two
dollars a week!" From this feeble joke the most foolish
tales have arisen, and grown in the retelling, of his having
been a reporter connected with a San Francisco paper. The
Monterey Californian was a tiny sheet that was hardly in
a position to pay any one so much as two dollars a week.
The editor was also the printer and did all the work on

his paper with his own hands. The idea of a reporter in a place where "the population is about that of a dissenting chapel on a wet Sunday...mostly Mexican and Indian," was thought very amusing by both my husband and Mr. Bronson, the editor, but some one seems to have taken it very seriously.

The Amateur Emigrant was partly written in Monterey, and almost finished in San Francisco under the most depressing circumstances of ill health, poverty, and letters of adverse criticism from friends in England. In an unfinished letter dated Calistoga, June 4, 1880, he writes: "Today at last I send the last of the Double Damned Emigrant. It was all written, after a fashion, months ago, before I caved in; yet I have not had the pluck and strength to finish copying these few sheets before to-day. The attempt has cost me many a heavy heart....I have done a quaint action—I have sent three of my poems to the *Atlantic Monthly*, and a fourth, heaven of heavens! to Stephen![1] I am not mad; only a poet."

F. V. DE G. S.

[1] Leslie Stephen, at that time editing an English magazine.

DEDICATION

TO

ROBERT ALAN MOWBRAY STEVENSON

Our friendship was not only founded before we were born by a community of blood, but is in itself near as old as my life. It began with our early ages, and, like a history, has been continued to the present time. Although we may not be old in the world, we are old to each other, having so long been intimates. We are now widely separated, a great sea and continent intervening ; but memory, like care, mounts into iron ships and rides post behind the horseman. Neither time nor space nor enmity can conquer old affection ; and as I dedicate these sketches, it is not to you only but to all in the old country, that I send the greeting of my heart.

R. L. S.

1879.

The Amateur Emigrant

THE SECOND CABIN

I FIRST encountered my fellow-passengers on the Broomielaw in Glasgow. Thence we descended the Clyde in no familiar spirit, but looking askance on each other as on possible enemies. A few Scandinavians, who had already grown acquainted on the North Sea, were friendly and voluble over their long pipes ; but among English speakers distance and suspicion reigned supreme. The sun was soon overclouded, the wind freshened and grew sharp as we continued to descend the widening estuary ; and with the falling temperature the gloom among the passengers increased. Two of the women wept. Any one who had come aboard might have supposed we were all absconding from the law. There was scarce a word interchanged, and no common sentiment but that of cold united us, until at length, having touched at Greenock, a pointing arm and a rush to the starboard now announced that our ocean steamer was in sight. There she lay in mid-river, at the tail of the Bank, her sea-signal flying : a wall of bulwark, a street of white deck-houses, an aspiring forest of spars, larger than a church, and soon to be as populous as many an incorporated town in the land to which she was to bear us.

I was not, in truth, a steerage passenger.
Although anxious to see the worst of emigrant
life, I had some work to finish on the voyage,
and was advised to go by the second cabin,
where at least I should have a table at command.
The advice was excellent ; but to understand
the choice, and what I gained, some outline of
the internal disposition of the ship will first be
necessary.   In her very nose is Steerage No. 1,
down two pair of stairs.   A little abaft, another
companion, labelled Steerage No. 2 and 3, gives
admission to three galleries, two running forward
towards Steerage No. 1, and the third aft towards
the engines.   The starboard forward gallery is
the second cabin.   Away abaft the engines and
below the officers' cabins, to complete our survey
of the vessel, there is yet a third nest of steerages,
labelled 4 and 5.   The second cabin, to return,
is thus a modified oasis in the very heart of the
steerages.   Through the thin partition you can
hear the steerage passengers being sick, the rattle
of tin dishes as they sit at meals, the varied
accents in which they converse, the crying of
their children terrified by this new experience, or
the clean flat smack of the parental hand in
chastisement.

There are, however, many advantages for the
inhabitant of this strip.   He does not require to
bring his own bedding or dishes, but finds berths
and a table completely if somewhat roughly
furnished.   He enjoys a distinct superiority in
diet ; but this, strange to say, differs not only

on different ships, but on the same ship according as her head is to the east or west. In my own experience, the principal difference between out table and that of the true steerage passenger was the table itself, and the crockery plates from which we ate. But lest I should show myself ungrateful, let me recapitulate every advantage. At breakfast, we had a choice between tea and coffee for beverage ; a choice. not easy to make, the two were so surprisingly alike. I found that I could sleep after the coffee and lay awake after the tea, which is proof conclusive of some chemical disparity ; and even by the palate I could distinguish a smack of snuff in the former from a flavour of boiling and dishcloths in the second. As a matter of fact, I have seen passengers, after many sips, still doubting which had been supplied them. In the way of eatables at the same meal we were gloriously favoured ; for in addition to porridge. which was common to all, we had Irish stew, sometimes a bit of fish, and sometimes rissoles. The dinner of soup, roast fresh beef, boiled salt junk, and potatoes, was, I believe, exactly common to the steerage and the second cabin ; only I have heard it rumoured that our potatoes were of a superior brand ; and twice a week, on pudding-days, instead of duff, we had a saddlebag filled with currants under the name of a plum-pudding. At tea we were served with some broken meat from the saloon ; sometimes in the comparatively elegant form of spare patties or rissoles ; but as a general thing, mere chicken-bones and flakes of fish, neither hot nor cold. If these were not the scrapings of plates their looks belied them sorely ; yet we were all too hungry to be proud, and fell to these leavings greedily. These, the bread, which was excellent, and the soup and porridge, which were both good, formed my whole diet throughout the voyage ; so that except for the broken meat and the convenience of a table I might as well have been in the steerage outright. Had they given me porridge again in the evening, I should have been perfectly contented with the fare. As it was, with a few biscuits and some whisky and water before turning in, I kept my body going and my spirits up to the mark.

The last particular in which the second-cabin passenger remarkably stands ahead of his brother of the steerage is one altogether of sentiment. In the steerage there are males and females ; in the second cabin ladies and gentlemen. For some time after I came aboard I thought I was only a male ; but in the course of a voyage of discovery between decks, I came on a brass plate, and learned that I was still a gentleman. Nobody knew it, of course. I was lost in the crowd of males and females, and rigorously confined to the same quarter of the deck. Who could tell whether I housed on the port or starboard side of Steerage No. 2 and 3 ? And it was only there that my superiority became practical ; everywhere else I was incognito, moving among my inferiors with simplicity, not so much as a swagger to indicate that I was a gentleman after all, and had broken meat to tea. Still, I was like one with a patent of nobility in a drawer at home ; and when I felt out of spirits I could go down and refresh myself with a look of that brass plate.

For all these advantages I paid but two guineas. Six guineas is the steerage fare ; eight that by the second cabin ; and when you remember that the steerage passenger must supply bedding and dishes, and, in five cases out of ten, either brings some dainties with him, or privately pays the steward for extra rations, the difference in price becomes almost nominal. Air comparatively fit to breathe, food comparatively varied, and the satisfaction of being still privately a gentleman, may thus be had almost for the asking. Two of my fellow-passengers in the second cabin had already made the passage by the cheaper fare, and declared it was an experiment not to be repeated. As I go on to tell about my steerage friends, the reader will perceive that they were not alone in their opinion. Out of ten with whom I was more or less intimate, I am sure not fewer than five vowed, if they returned, to travel second cabin ; and all who had left their wives behind them assured me they would go without the comfort of their presence until they could afford to bring them by saloon.

Our party in the second cabin was not perhaps the most interesting on board. Perhaps even in

the saloon there was as much goodwill and
character.   Yet it had some elements of curiosity.
There was a mixed group of Swedes, Danes and
Norsemen, one of whom, generally known by the
name of " Johnny," in spite of his own protests,
greatly diverted us by his clever, cross-country
efforts to speak English, and became on the
strength of that an universal favourite—it takes
so little in this world of shipboard to create a
popularity.   There was, besides, a Scots mason,
known from his favourite dish as " Irish Stew,"
three or four nondescript Scots, a fine young
Irishman, O'Reilly, and a pair of young men
who deserve a special word of condemnation.
One of them was Scots ; the other claimed to be
American ; admitted, after some fencing, that
he was born in England ; and ultimately proved
to be an Irishman born and nurtured, but
ashamed to own his country.   He has a sister on
board, whom he faithfully neglected throughout
the voyage, though she was not only sick, but
much his senior, and had nursed and cared for
him in childhood.   In appearance he was like
an imbecile Henry the Third of France.   The
Scotsman, though perhaps as big an ass, was not
so dead of heart ; and I have only bracketed
them together because they were fast friends,
and disgraced themselves equally by their conduct at the table.

Next, to turn to topics more agreeable, we
had a newly married couple, devoted to each
other, with a pleasant story of how they had

first seen each other years ago at a preparatory school, and that very afternoon he had carried her books home for her. I do not know if this story will be plain to Southern readers; but to me it recalls many a school idyll, with wrathful swains of eight and nine confronting each other stride-legs, flushed with jealousy; for to carry home a young lady's books was both a delicate attention and a privilege.

Then there was an old lady, or indeed I am not sure that she was as much old as antiquated and strangely out of place, who had left her husband, and was travelling all the way to Kansas by herself. We had to take her own word that she was married; for it was sorely contradicted by the testimony of her appearance. Nature seemed to have sanctified her for the single state; even the colour of her hair was incompatible with matrimony, and her husband, I thought, should be a man of saintly spirit and phantasmal bodily presence. She was ill, poor thing; her soul turned from the viands; the dirty tablecloth shocked her like an impropriety; and the whole strength of her endeavour was bent upon keeping her watch true to Glasgow time till she should reach New York. They had heard reports, her husband and she, of some unwarrantable disparity of hours between these two cities; and with a spirit commendably scientific, had seized on this occasion to put them to the proof. It was a good thing for the old lady; for she passed much leisure time in studying the watch. Once, when prostrated by sickness, she let it run down. It was inscribed on her harmless mind in letters of adamant that the hands of a watch must never be turned backwards; and so it behoved her to lie in wait for the exact moment ere she started it again. When she imagined this was about due, she sought out one of the young second-cabin Scotsmen, who was embarked on the same experiment as herself and had hitherto been less neglectful. She was in quest of two o'clock; and when she learned it was already seven on the shores of Clyde, she lifted up her voice and cried "Gravy!" I had not heard this innocent expletive since I was a young child; and I suppose it must have been the same with the other Scotsman present, for we all laughed our fill.

Last but not least, I come to my excellent friend Mr. Jones. It would be difficult to say whether I was his right-hand man, or he mine, during the voyage. Thus at table I carved, while he only scooped gravy; but at our concerts, of which more anon, he was the president who called up performers to sing, and I but his messenger who ran his errands and pleaded privately with the over-modest. I knew I liked Mr. Jones from the moment I saw him. I thought him by his face to be Scottish; nor could his accent undeceive me. For as there is a *lingua franca* of many tongues on the moles and in the feluccas of the Mediterranean, so there is a free or common accent among English-

speaking men who follow the sea. They catch a
twang in a New England port ; from a cockney
skipper, even a Scotsman sometimes learns to
drop an *h ;* a word of a dialect is picked up from
another hand in the forecastle ; until often the
result is undecipherable, and you have to ask for
the man's place of birth. So it was with Mr.
Jones. I thought him a Scotsman who had
been long to sea ; and yet he was from Wales,
and had been most of his life a blacksmith at
an inland forge ; a few years in America and
half a score of ocean voyages having sufficed to
modify his speech into the common pattern. By
his own account he was both strong and skilful
in his trade. A few years back, he had been
married and after a fashion a rich man ; now the
wife was dead and the money gone. But his
was the nature that looks forward, and goes on
from one year to another and through all the
extremities of fortune undismayed ; and if the
sky were to fall to-morrow, I should look to see
Jones, the day following, perched on a step-ladder
and getting things to rights. He was always
hovering round inventions like a bee over a
flower, and lived in a dream of patents. He had
with him a patent medicine, for instance, the
composition of which he had bought years ago
for five dollars from an American pedlar, and
sold the other day for a hundred pounds (I think
it was) to an English apothecary. It was called
Golden Oil : cured all maladies without exception ; and I am bound to say that I partook of

it myself with good results. It is a character of
the man that he was not only perpetually dosing
himself with Golden Oil, but wherever there was
a head aching or a finger cut, there would be
Jones with his bottle.

If he had one taste more strongly than another,
it was to study character. Many an hour have
we two walked upon the deck dissecting our
neighbours in a spirit that was too purely scientific
to be called unkind ; whenever a quaint or human
trait slipped out in conversation, you might
have seen Jones and me exchanging glances ; and
we could hardly go to bed in comfort till we had
exchanged notes and discussed the day's experience. We were then like a couple of anglers
comparing a day's kill. But the fish we angled
for were of a metaphysical species, and we
angled as often as not in one another's baskets.
Once, in the midst of a serious talk, each found
there was a scrutinising eye upon himself ; I
own I paused in embarrassment at this double
detection ; but Jones, with a better civility,
broke into a peal of unaffected laughter, and
declared, what was the truth, that there was a
pair of us indeed.

EARLY IMPRESSIONS

WE steamed out of the Clyde on Thursday night, and early on the Friday afternoon we took in our last batch of emigrants at Lough Foyle, in Ireland, and said farewell to Europe. The company was now complete, and began to draw together, by inscrutable magnetisms, upon the decks. There were Scots and Irish in plenty, a few English, a few Americans, a good handful of Scandinavians, a German or two, and one Russian; all now belonging for ten days to one small iron country on the deep.

As I walked the deck and looked round upon my fellow-passengers, thus curiously assorted from all northern Europe, I began for the first time to understand the nature of emigration. Day by day throughout the passage, and thenceforward across all the States, and on to the shores of the Pacific, this knowledge grew more clear and melancholy. Emigration, from a word of the most cheerful import, came to sound most dismally in my ear. There is nothing more agreeable to picture and nothing more pathetic to behold. The abstract idea, as conceived at home, is hopeful and adventurous. A young man, you fancy, scorning restraints and helpers, issues forth into life, that great battle, to fight for his own hand. The most pleasant stories of ambition, of difficulties overcome, and of ultimate success, are but as episodes to this great epic of self-help. The epic is composed of individual heroisms ; it stands to them as the victorious war which subdued an empire stands to the personal act of bravery which spiked a single cannon and was adequately rewarded with a medal. For in emigration the young men enter direct and by the shipload on their heritage of work ; empty continents swarm, as at the bo's'un's whistle, with industrious hands, and whole new empires are domesticated to the service of man.

This is the closet picture, and is found, on trial, to consist mostly of embellishments. The more I saw of my fellow-passengers, the less I was tempted to the lyric note. Comparatively few of the men were below thirty ; many were married, and encumbered with families ; not a few were already up in years ; and this itself was out of tune with my imaginations, for the ideal emigrant should certainly be young. Again, I thought he should offer to the eye some bold type of humanity, with bluff or hawk-like features, and the stamp of an eager and pushing disposition. Now those around me were for the most part quiet, orderly, obedient citizens, family men broken by adversity, elderly youths who had failed to place themselves in life, and people who had seen better days. Mildness was the prevailing character ; mild mirth and mild endurance. In a word, I was not taking part in an impetuous and conquering sally, such as swept over Mexico or Siberia, but found myself, like Marmion, " in the lost battle, borne down by the flying."

Labouring mankind had in the last years, and throughout Great Britain, sustained a prolonged and crushing series of defeats. I had heard vaguely of these reverses ; of whole streets of houses standing deserted by the Tyne, the cellar-doors broken and removed for firewood ; of homeless men loitering at the street-corners of Glasgow with their chests beside them ; of closed factories, useless strikes, and starving girls. But I had never taken them home to me or represented these distresses livingly to my imagination. A turn of the market may be a calamity as disastrous as the French retreat from Moscow ; but it hardly lends itself to lively treatment, and makes a trifling figure in the morning papers. We may struggle as we please, we are not born economists. The individual is more affecting than the mass. It is by the scenic accidents, and the appeal to the carnal eye, that for the most part we grasp the significance of tragedies. Thus it was only now, when I found myself involved in the rout, that I began to appreciate how sharp had been the battle. We were a company of the rejected ; the drunken, the incompetent, the weak, the prodigal, all who had been unable to prevail against circumstances in the one land, were now fleeing pitifully to

another ; and though one or two might still
succeed, all had already failed. We were a
shipful of failures, the broken men of England.
Yet it must not be supposed that these people
exhibited depression. The scene, on the contrary, was cheerful. Not a tear was shed on
board the vessel. All were full of hope for the
future, and showed an inclination to innocent
gaiety. Some were heard to sing, and all began
to scrape acquaintance with small jests and
ready laughter.

The children found each other out like dogs,
and ran about the decks scraping acquaintance
after their fashion also. " What do you call
your mither ? " I heard one ask. " Mawmaw,"
was the reply, indicating, I fancy, a shade of
difference in the social scale. When people pass
each other on the high seas of life at so early an
age, the contact is but slight, and the relation
more like what we may imagine to be the friendship of flies than that of men ; it is so quickly
joined, so easily dissolved, so open in its com-
munications and so devoid of deeper human
qualities. The children, I observed, were all in
a band, and as thick as thieves at a fair, while
their elders were still ceremoniously manœuvring
on the outskirts of acquaintance. The sea, the
ship, and the seamen were soon as familiar as
home to these half-conscious little ones. It was
odd to hear them, throughout the voyage,
employ shore words to designate portions of
the vessel. " Co' 'way doon to yon dyke," I

heard one say, probably meaning the bulwark.
I often had my heart in my mouth, watching
them climb into the shrouds or on the rails,
while the ship went swinging through the waves ;
and I admired and envied the courage of their
mothers, who sat by in the sun and looked on
with composure at these perilous feats. " He'll
maybe be a sailor," I heard one remark ; " now's
the time to learn."   I had been on the point of
running forward to interfere, but stood back at
that, reproved. Very few in the more delicate
classes have the nerve to look upon the peril of
one dear to them ; but the life of poorer folk,
where necessity is so much more immediate and
imperious, braces even a mother to this extreme
of endurance. And perhaps, after all, it is better
that the lad should break his neck than that you
should break his spirit.

   And since I am here on the chapter of the
children, I must mention one little fellow, whose
family belonged to Steerage No. 4 and 5, and who,
wherever he went, was like a strain of music
round the ship. He was an ugly, merry, unbreeched child of three, his lint-white hair in a
tangle, his face smeared with suet and treacle ;
but he ran to and fro with so natural a step, and
fell and picked himself up again with such grace
and good-humour, that he might fairly be called
beautiful when he was in motion. To meet him,
crowing with laughter and beating an accompaniment to his own mirth with a tin spoon upon
a tin cup, was to meet a little triumph of the

human species.   Even when his mother and the
rest of his family lay sick and prostrate around
him, he sat upright in their midst and sang aloud
in the pleasant heartlessness of infancy.

Throughout the Friday, intimacy among us
men made but a few advances. We discussed
the probable duration of the voyage, we exchanged pieces of information, naming our
trades, what we hoped to find in the new world,
or what we were fleeing from in the old ; and,
above all, we condoled together over the food
and the vileness of the steerage. One or two
had been so near famine that you may say they
had run into the ship with the devil at their
heels ; and to these all seemed for the best in
the best of possible steamers. But the majority
were hugely discontented. Coming as they did
from a country is so low a state as Great Britain,
many of them from Glasgow, which commer-
cially speaking was as good as dead, and many
having long been out of work, I was surprised to
find them so dainty in their notions. I myself
lived almost exclusively on bread, porridge, and
soup, precisely as it was supplied to them, and
found it, if not luxurious, at least sufficient.
But these working men were loud in their outcries. It was not " food for human beings," it
was " only fit for pigs," it was " a disgrace."
Many of them lived almost entirely upon biscuit,
others on their own private supplies, and some
paid extra for better rations from the ship.
This marvellously changed my notion of the

degree of luxury habitual to the artisan. I was prepared to hear him grumble, for grumbling is the traveller's pastime ; but I was not prepared to find him turn away from a diet which was palatable to myself. Words I should have disregarded, or taken with a liberal allowance ; but when a man prefers dry biscuit there can be no question of the sincerity of his disgust.

With one of their complaints I could most heartily sympathise. A single night of the steerage had filled them with horror. I had myself suffered, even in my decent second-cabin berth, from the lack of air ; and as the night promised to be fine and quiet, I determined to sleep on deck, and advised all who complained of their quarters to follow my example. I daresay a dozen of others agreed to do so, and I thought we should have been quite a party. Yet, when I brought up my rug about seven bells, there was no one to be seen but the watch. That chimerical terror of good night-air, which makes men close their windows, list their doors, and seal themselves up with their own poisonous exhalations, had sent all these healthy workmen down below. One would think we had been brought up in a fever country ; yet in England the most malarious districts are in the bed-chambers.

I felt saddened at this defection, and yet half-pleased to have the night so quietly to myself. The wind had hauled a little ahead on the starboard bow, and was dry but chilly. I found a shelter near the fire-hole, and made myself snug

for the night. The ship moved over the uneven
sea with a gentle and cradling movement. The
ponderous, organic labours of the engine in her
bowels occupied the mind, and prepared it for
slumber. From time to time a heavier lurch
would disturb me as I lay, and recall me to the
obscure borders of consciousness ; or I heard, as
it were through a veil, the clear note of the
clapper on the brass and the beautiful sea-cry,
" All's well ! " I know nothing, whether for
poetry or music, that can surpass the effect of these
two syllables in the darkness of a night at sea.

The day dawned fairly enough, and during the
early part we had some pleasant hours to improve
acquaintance in the open air ; but towards
nightfall the wind freshened, the rain began to
fall, and the sea rose so high that it was difficult
to keep one's footing on the deck. I have spoken
of our concerts. We were indeed a musical
ship's company, and cheered our way into exile
with the fiddle, the accordion, and the songs of
all nations. Good, bad, or indifferent—Scottish,
English, Irish, Russian, German, or Norse—the
songs were received with generous applause.
Once or twice a recitation, very spiritedly rendered in a powerful Scottish accent, varied the
proceedings ; and once we sought in vain to
dance a quadrille, eight men of us together, to
the music of the violin. The performers were
all humorous, frisky fellows, who loved to cut
capers in private life ; but as soon as they were
arranged for the dance, they conducted them-

selves like so many mutes at a funeral. I have never seen decorum pushed so far; and as this was not expected, the quadrille was soon whistled down, and the dancers departed under a cloud. Eight Frenchmen, even eight Englishmen from another rank of society, would have dared to make some fun for themselves and the spectators; but the working man, when sober, takes an extreme and even melancholy view of personal deportment. A fifth-form schoolboy is not more careful of dignity. He dares not be comical; his fun must escape from him unprepared, and above all, it must be unaccompanied by any physical demonstration. I like his society under most circumstances, but let me never again join with him in public gambols.

But the impulse to sing was strong, and triumphed over modesty and even the inclemencies of sea and sky. On this rough Saturday night, we got together by the main deck-house, in a place sheltered from the wind and rain. Some clinging to a ladder which led to the hurricane deck, and the rest knitting arms or taking hands, we made a ring to support the women in the violent lurching of the ship; and when we were thus disposed, sang to our heart's content. Some of the songs were appropriate to the scene; others strikingly the reverse. Bastard doggerel of the music-hall, such as, " Around her splendid form, I weaved the magic circle," sounded bald, bleak, and pitifully silly. " We don't want to fight, but, by Jingo, if we do," was in some

measure saved by the vigour and unanimity
with which the chorus was thrown forth into the
night. I observed a Platt-Deutsch mason, entirely innocent of English, adding heartily to
the general effect. And perhaps the German
mason is but a fair example of the sincerity with
which the song was rendered; for nearly all
with whom I conversed upon the subject were
bitterly opposed to war, and attributed their
own misfortunes, and frequently their own taste
for whisky, to the campaigns in Zululand and
Afghanistan.

Every now and again, however, some song that
touched the pathos of our situation was given
forth; and you could hear by the voices that
took up the burden how the sentiment came
home to each. "The Anchor's Weighed" was
true for us. We were indeed "Rocked on the
bosom of the stormy deep." How many of us
could say with the singer, "I'm lonely to-night,
love, without you," or "Go, some one, and tell
them from me, to write me a letter from home!"
And when was there a more appropriate moment
for "Auld Lang Syne" than now, when the
land, the friends, and the affections of that
mingled but beloved time were fading and fleeing
behind us in the vessel's wake? It pointed forward to the hour when these labours should be
overpast, to the return voyage, and to many a
meeting in the sanded inn, when those who had
parted in the spring of youth should again drink
a cup of kindness in their age. Had not Burns

contemplated emigration, I scarce believe he would have found that note.

All Sunday the weather remained wild and cloudy, many were prostrated by sickness; only five sat down to tea in the second cabin, and two of these departed abruptly ere the meal was at an end. The Sabbath was observed strictly by the majority of the emigrants. I heard an old woman express her surprise that " the ship didna gae doon," as she saw someone pass her with a chess-board on the holy day. Some sang Scottish psalms. Many went to service, and in true Scottish fashion came back ill-pleased with their divine. " I didna think he was an experienced preacher," said one girl to me.

It was a bleak, uncomfortable day; but at night, by six bells, although the wind had not yet moderated, the clouds were all wrecked and blown away behind the rim of the horizon, and the stars came out thickly overhead. I saw Venus burning as steadily and sweetly across this hurly-burly of the winds and waters as ever at home upon the summer woods. The engine pounded, the screw tossed out of the water with a roar, and shook the ship from end to end; the bows battled with loud reports against the billows : and as I stood in the lee-scuppers and looked up to where the funnel leaned out, over my head, vomiting smoke, and the black and monstrous topsails blotted, at each lurch, a different crop of stars, it seemed as if all this trouble were a thing of small account, and that just above the mast reigned peace unbroken and eternal.

STEERAGE SCENES

OUR companion (Steerage No. 2 and 3) was a favourite resort. Down one flight of stairs there was a comparatively large open space, the centre occupied by a hatchway, which made a convenient seat for about twenty persons, while barrels, coils of rope, and the carpenter's bench afforded perches for perhaps as many more. The canteen, or steerage bar, was on one side of the stair; on the other, a no less attractive spot, the cabin of the indefatigable interpreter. I have seen people packed into this space like herrings in a barrel, and many merry evenings prolonged there until five bells, when the lights were ruthlessly extinguished and all must go to roost.

It had been rumoured since Friday that there was a fiddler aboard, who lay sick and un-melodious in Steerage No. 1; and on the Monday forenoon, as I came down the companion, I was saluted by something in Strathspey time. A white-faced Orpheus was cheerily playing to an audience of white-faced women. It was as much as he could do to play, and some of his hearers were scarce able to sit; yet they had crawled from their bunks at the first experimental flourish, and found better than medicine in the music. Some of the heaviest heads began to nod in time, and a degree of animation looked from some of the palest eyes. Humanly speaking, it is a more important matter to play the fiddle, even badly, than to write huge works upon recondite subjects. What could Mr. Darwin have done for these sick women ? But this fellow scraped away ; and the world was positively a better place for all who heard him. We have yet to understand the economical value of these mere accomplishments. I told the fiddler he was a happy man, carrying happiness about with him in his fiddle-case, and he seemed alive to the fact.

" It is a privilege," I said. He thought a while upon the word, turning it over in his Scots head, and then answered with conviction, " Yes, a privilege."

That night I was summoned by " Merrily danced the Quaker's wife " into the companion of Steerage No. 4 and 5. This was, properly speaking, but a strip across a deck-house, lit by a sickly lantern which swung to and fro with the motion of the ship. Through the open slide-door we had a glimpse of a grey night sea, with patches of phosphorescent foam flying, swift as birds, into the wake, and the horizon rising and falling as the vessel rolled to the wind. In the centre the companion ladder plunged down sheerly like an open pit. Below, on the first landing, and lighted by another lamp, lads and lasses danced, not more than three at a time for lack of space, in jigs and reels and hornpipes.

Above, on either side, there was a recess railed
with iron, perhaps two feet wide and four long,
which stood for orchestra and seats of honour.
In the one balcony, five slatternly Irish lasses
sat woven in a comely group. In the other was
posted Orpheus, his body, which was convulsively
in motion, forming an odd contrast to his somno-
lent, imperturbable Scots face. His brother, a
dark man with a vehement, interested countenance, who made a god of the fiddler, sat by with
open mouth, drinking in the general admiration
and throwing out remarks to kindle it.

" That's a bonny hornpipe now," he would
say, " it's a great favourite with performers ;
they dance the sand dance to it." And he ex-
pounded the sand dance. Then suddenly, it
would be a long " Hush ! " with uplifted finger
and glowing, supplicating eyes ; " he's going to
play ' Auld Robin Gray ' on one string ! " And
throughout this excruciating movement—" On
one string, that's on one string ! " he kept crying.
I would have given something myself that it
had been on none ; but the hearers were much
awed. I called for a tune or two, and thus
introduced myself to the notice of the brother,
who directed his talk to me for some little while,
keeping, I need hardly mention, true to his topic,
like the seamen to the star. " He's grand of it,"
he said confidentially. " His master was a
music-hall man." Indeed the music-hall man
had left his mark, for our fiddler was ignorant
of many of our best old airs ; " Logie o' Buchan,"

for instance, he only knew as a quick, jigging figure in a set of quadrilles, and had never heard it called by name. Perhaps, after all, the brother was the more interesting performer of the two. I have spoken with him afterwards repeatedly, and found him always the same quick, fiery bit of a man, not without brains; but he never showed to such advantage as when he was thus squiring the fiddler into public note. There is nothing more becoming than a genuine admiration; and it shares this with love, that it does not become contemptible although misplaced.

The dancing was but feebly carried on. The space was almost impracticably small; and the Irish wenches combined the extreme of bashfulness about this innocent display with a surprising impudence and roughness of address. Most often, either the fiddle lifted up its voice unheeded, or only a couple of lads would be footing it and snapping fingers on the landing. And such was the eagerness of the brother to display all the acquirements of his idol, and such the sleepy indifference of the performer, that the tune would as often as not be changed, and the hornpipe expire into a ballad before the dancers had cut half a dozen shuffles.

In the meantime, however, the audience had been growing more and more numerous every moment; there was hardly standing-room round the top of the companion; and the strange instinct of the race moved some of the new-comers to close both the doors, so that the atmosphere grew insupportable. It was a good place, as the saying is, to leave.

The wind hauled ahead with a head sea. By ten at night heavy sprays were flying and drumming over the forecastle; the companion of Steerage No. 1 had to be closed, and the door of communication through the second cabin thrown open. Either from the convenience of the opportunity, or because we had already a number of acquaintances in that part of the ship, Mr. Jones and I paid it a late visit. Steerage No. 1 is shaped like an isosceles triangle, the sides opposite the equal angles bulging outward with the contour of the ship. It is lined with eight pens of sixteen bunks apiece, four bunks below and four above on either side. At night the place is lit with two lanterns, one to each table. As the steamer beat on her way among the rough billows, the light passed through violent phases of change, and was thrown to and fro and up and down with startling swiftness. You were tempted to wonder, as you looked, how so thin a glimmer could control and disperse such solid blackness. When Jones and I entered we found a little company of our acquaintances seated together at the triangular foremost table. A more forlorn party, in more dismal circumstances, it would be hard to imagine. The motion here in the ship's nose was very violent; the uproar of the sea often overpoweringly loud. The yellow flicker of the lantern spun round and round and tossed the shadows in masses. The air was hot, but it struck a chill from its fœtor. From all round in the dark bunks, the scarcely human noises of the sick joined into a kind of farmyard chorus. In the midst, these five friends of mine were keeping up what heart they could in company. Singing was their refuge from discomfortable thoughts and sensations. One piped, in feeble tones, " O why left I my hame ? " which seemed a pertinent question in the circumstances. Another, from the invisible horrors of a pen where he lay dog-sick upon the upper shelf, found courage, in a blink of his sufferings, to give us several verses of the " Death of Nelson " ; and it was odd and eerie to hear the chorus breathe feebly from all sorts of dark corners, and " this day has done his dooty " rise and fall and be taken up again in this dim *inferno*, to an accompaniment of plunging, hollow-sounding bows and the rattling spray-showers overhead.

All seemed unfit for conversation ; a certain dizziness had interrupted the activity of their minds ; and except to sing they were tongue-tied. There was present, however, one tall, powerful fellow of doubtful nationality, being neither quite Scotsman nor altogether Irish, but of surprising clearness of conviction on the highest problems. He had gone nearly beside himself on the Sunday, because of a general backwardness to indorse his definition of mind as " a living, thinking substance which cannot be felt, heard, or seen "—nor, I presume, although he failed to mention it, smelt. Now he came

forward in a pause with another contribution to
our culture.

" Just by way of change," said he, " I'll ask
you a Scripture riddle. There's profit in them
too," he added ungrammatically.

This was the riddle—

> C and P
> Did agree
> To cut down C ;
> But C and P
> Could not agree
> Without the leave of G,
> All the people cried to see
> The crueltie
> Of C and P.

Harsh are the words of Mercury after the songs
of Apollo ! We were a long while over the problem, shaking our heads and gloomily wondering
how a man could be such a fool ; but at length
he put us out of suspense and divulged the fact
that C and P stood for Caiaphas and Pontius
Pilate.

I think it must have been the riddle that settled
us ; but the motion and the close air likewise
hurried our departure. We had not been gone
long, we heard next morning, ere two or even
three out of the five fell sick. We thought it
little wonder on the whole, for the sea kept
contrary all night. I now made my bed upon
the second cabin floor, where, although I ran the
risk of being stepped upon, I had a free current
of air, more or less vitiated indeed, and running

only from steerage to steerage, but at least not stagnant; and from this couch, as well as the usual sounds of a rough night at sea, the hateful coughing and retching of the sick and the sobs of children, I heard a man run wild with terror beseeching his friend for encouragement. "The ship's going down!" he cried with a thrill of agony. "The ship's going down!" he repeated, now in a blank whisper, now with his voice rising towards a sob; and his friend might reassure him, reason with him, joke at him— all was in vain, and the old cry came back, "The ship's going down!" There was something panicky and catching in the emotion of his tones; and I saw in a clear flash what an involved and hideous tragedy was a disaster to an emigrant ship. If this whole parishful of people came no more to land, into how many houses would the newspaper carry woe, and what a great part of the web of our corporate human life would be rent across for ever!

The next morning when I came on deck I found a new world indeed. The wind was fair; the sun mounted into a cloudless heaven; through great dark blue seas the ship cut a swath of curded foam. The horizon was dotted all day with companionable sails, and the sun shone pleasantly on the long, heaving deck.

We had many fine-weather diversions to beguile the time. There was a single chess-board and a single pack of cards. Sometimes as many as twenty of us would be playing dominoes for love. Feats of dexterity, puzzles for the intelligence, some arithmetical, some of the same order as the old problem of the fox and goose and cabbage, were always welcome; and the latter, I observed, more popular as well as more conspicuously well done than the former. We had a regular daily competition to guess the vessel's progress; and twelve o'clock, when the result was published in the wheel-house, came to be a moment of considerable interest. But the interest was unmixed. Not a bet was laid upon our guesses. From the Clyde to Sandy Hook I never heard a wager offered or taken. We had, besides, romps in plenty. Puss in the Corner, which we had rebaptised, in more manly style, Devil and four Corners, was my own favourite game; but there were many who preferred another, the humour of which was to box a person's ears until he found out who had cuffed him.

This Tuesday morning we were all delighted with the change of weather, and in the highest possible spirits. We got in a cluster like bees, sitting between each other's feet under lee of the deck-houses. Stories and laughter went around. The children climbed about the shrouds. White faces appeared for the first time, and began to take on colour from the wind. I was kept hard at work making cigarettes for one amateur after another, and my less than moderate skill was heartily admired. Lastly, down sat the fiddler in our midst and began to discourse his reels, and jigs, and ballads, with now and then a voice or two to take up the air and throw in the interest of human speech.

Through this merry and good-hearted scene there came three cabin passengers, a gentleman and two young ladies, picking their way with little gracious titters of indulgence, and a Lady-Bountiful air about nothing, which galled me to the quick. I have little of the radical in social questions, and have always nourished an idea that one person was as good as another. But I began to be troubled by this episode. It was astonishing what insults these people managed to convey by their presence. They seemed to throw their clothes in our faces. Their eyes searched us all over for tatters and incongruities. A laugh was ready at their lips ; but they were too well-mannered to indulge it in our hearing. Wait a bit, till they were all back in the saloon, and then hear how wittily they would depict the manners of the steerage. We were in truth very innocently, cheerfully, and sensibly engaged, and there was no shadow of excuse for the swaying elegant superiority with which these damsels passed among us, or for the stiff and waggish glances of their squire. Not a word was said ; only when they were gone Mackay sullenly damned their impudence under his breath ; but we were all conscious of an icy influence and a dead break in the course of our enjoyment.

STEERAGE TYPES

WE had a fellow on board, an Irish-American, for all the world like a beggar in a print by Callot ; one-eyed, with great, splay, crow's-feet round the sockets ; a knotty squab nose coming down over his moustache ; a miraculous hat ; a shirt that had been white, ay, ages long ago ; an alpaca coat in its last sleeves ; and, without hyperbole, no buttons to his trousers. Even in these rags and tatters, the man twinkled all over with impudence like a piece of sham jewellery ; and I have heard him offer a situation to one of his fellow-passengers with the air of a lord. Nothing could overlie such a fellow ; a kind of base success was written on his brow. He was then in his ill days ; but I can imagine him in Congress with his mouth full of bombast and sawder. As we moved in the same circle, I was brought necessarily into his society. I do not think I ever heard him say anything that was true, kind, or interesting ; but there was entertainment in the man's demeanour. You might call him a half-educated Irish Tigg.

Our Russian made a remarkable contrast to this impossible fellow. Rumours and legends were current in the steerages about his antecedents. Some said he was a Nihilist escaping ;

others set him down for a harmless spendthrift, who had squandered fifty thousand roubles, and whose father had now despatched him to America by way of penance. Either tale might flourish in security; there was no contradiction to be feared, for the hero spoke not one word of English. I got on with him lumberingly enough in broken German, and learnt from his own lips that he had been an apothecary. He carried the photograph of his betrothed in a pocket-book, and remarked that it did not do her justice. The cut of his head stood out from among the passengers; with an air of startling strangeness. The first natural instinct was to take him for a desperado; but although the features, to our Western eyes, had a barbaric and unhomely cast, the eye both reassured and touched. It was large and very dark and soft, with an expression of dumb endurance, as if it had often looked on desperate circumstances and never looked on them without resolution.

He cried out when I used the word. " No, no," he said, " not resolution."

" The resolution to endure," I explained.

And then he shrugged his shoulders, and said, " *Ach, ja,*" with gusto, like a man who has been flattered in his favourite pretensions. Indeed, he was always hinting at some secret sorrow; and his life, he said, had been one of unusual trouble and anxiety; so the legends of the steerage may have represented at least some shadow of the truth. Once, and once only, he

sang a song at our concerts; standing forth
without embarrassment, his great stature somewhat humped, his long arms frequently extended,
his Kalmuck head thrown backward. It was a
suitable piece of music, as deep as a cow's bellow
and wild like the White Sea. He was struck and
charmed by the freedom and sociality of our
manners. At home, he said, no one on a journey
would speak to him, but those with whom he
would not care to speak; thus unconsciously
involving himself in the condemnation of his
countrymen. But Russia was soon to be changed;
the ice of the Neva was softening under the sun
of civilisation; the new ideas, "*wie ein feines
Violin*," were audible among the big empty
drum notes of Imperial diplomacy; and he
looked to see a great revival, though with a
somewhat indistinct and childish hope.

We had a father and son who made a pair of
Jacks-of-all-trades. It was the son who sang the
"Death of Nelson" under such contrarious
circumstances. He was by trade a shearer of
ship plates; but he could touch the organ, had
led two choirs, and played the flute and piccolo
in a professional string band. His repertory of
songs was, besides, inexhaustible, and ranged
impartially from the very best to the very worst
within his reach. Nor did he seem to make the
least distinction between these extremes, but
would cheerfully follow up "Tom Bowling"
with "Around her splendid form."

The father, an old, cheery, small piece of manhood, could do everything connected with tin-work from one end of the process to the other, use almost every carpenter's tool, and make picture frames to boot. " I sat down with silver plate every Sunday," said he, " and pictures on the wall. I have made enough money to be rolling in my carriage. But, sir," looking at me unsteadily with his bright rheumy eyes, " I was troubled with a drunken wife." He took a hostile view of matrimony in consequence. " It's an old saying," he remarked : " God made 'em, and the devil he mixed 'em."

I think he was justified by his experience. It was a dreary story. He would bring home three pounds on Saturday, and on Monday all the clothes would be in pawn. Sick of the useless struggle, he gave up a paying contract, and contented himself with small and ill-paid jobs. " A bad job was as good as a good job for me," he said ; " it all went the same way." Once the wife showed signs of amendment ; she kept steady for weeks on end ; it was again worth while to labour and to do one's best. The husband found a good situation some distance from home, and, to make a little upon every hand, started the wife in a cook-shop ; the children were here and there, busy as mice ; savings began to grow together in the bank, and the golden age of hope had returned again to that unhappy family. But one week my old acquaintance, getting earlier through with his work, came home on the Friday instead of the Saturday, and there

was his wife to receive him reeling drunk. He
" took and gave her a pair o' black eyes," for
which I pardon him, nailed up the cook-shop
door, gave up his situation, and resigned himself
to a life of poverty, with the workhouse at the
end. As the children came to their full age they
fled the house, and established themselves in
other countries ; some did well, some not so
well ; but the father remained at home alone
with his drunken wife, all his sound-hearted
pluck and varied accomplishments depressed and
negatived.

Was she dead now ? or, after all these years,
had he broken the chain, and run from home
like a schoolboy ? I could not discover which ;
but here at least he was out on the adventure,
and still one of the bravest and most youthful
men on board.

" Now, I suppose, I must put my old bones to
work again," said he ; " but I can do a turn
yet."

And the son to whom he was going, I asked,
was he not able to support him ?

" Oh yes," he replied. " But I'm never happy
without a job on hand. And I'm stout ; I can
eat a'most anything. You see no craze about
me."

This tale of a drunken wife was paralleled on
board by another of a drunken father. He was a
capable man, with a good chance in life ; but he
had drunk up two thriving businesses like a
bottle of sherry, and involved his sons along with

him in ruin. Now they were on board with us, fleeing his disastrous neighbourhood.

Total abstinence, like all ascetical conclusions, is unfriendly to the most generous, cheerful, and human parts of man ; but it could have adduced many instances and arguments from among our ship's company. I was one day conversing with a kind and happy Scotsman, running to fat and perspiration in the physical, but with a taste for poetry and a genial sense of fun. I had asked him his hopes in emigrating. They were like those of so many others, vague and unfounded ; times were bad at home ; they were said to have a turn for the better in the States ; and a man could get on anywhere, he thought. That was precisely the weak point of his position ; for if he could get on in America, why could he not do the same in Scotland ? But I never had the courage to use that argument, though it was often on the tip of my tongue, and instead I agreed with him heartily, adding, with reckless originality, " If the man stuck to his work, and kept away from drink."

" Ah ! " said he slowly, " the drink ! You see, that's just my trouble."

He spoke with a simplicity that was touching, looking at me at the same time with something strange and timid in his eye, half-ashamed, half-sorry, like a good child who knows he should be beaten. You would have said he recognised a destiny to which he was born, and accepted the consequences mildly. Like the merchant Abudah, he was at the same time fleeing from his destiny and carrying it along with him, the whole at an expense of six guineas.

As far as I saw, drink, idleness, and incompetency were the three great causes of emigration, and for all of them, and drink first and foremost, this trick of getting transported overseas appears to me the silliest means of cure. You cannot run away from a weakness ; you must some time fight it out or perish ; and if that be so, why not now, and where you stand ? *Cælum non animam.* Change Glenlivet for Bourbon, and it is still whisky, only not so good. A sea-voyage will not give a man the nerve to put aside cheap pleasure ; emigration has to be done before we climb the vessel ; an aim in life is the only fortune worth the finding ; and it is not to be found in foreign lands, but in the heart itself.

Speaking generally, there is no vice of this kind more contemptible than another ; for each is but a result and outward sign of a soul tragically shipwrecked. In the majority of cases, cheap pleasure is resorted to by way of anodyne. The pleasure-seeker sets forth upon life with high and difficult ambitions ; he meant to be nobly good and nobly happy, though at as little pains as possible to himself ; and it is because all has failed in his celestial enterprise that you now behold him rolling in the garbage. Hence the comparative success of the teetotal pledge ; because to a man who had nothing it sets at least a negative aim in life. Somewhat as prisoners beguile their days by taming a spider, the reformed drunkard makes an interest out of abstaining from intoxicating drinks, and may live for that negation. There is something, at least, *not to be done* each day ; and a cold triumph awaits him every evening.

We had one on board with us, whom I have already referred to under the name of Mackay, who seemed to me not only a good instance of this failure in life of which we have been speaking, but a good type of the intelligence which here surrounded me. Physically he was a small Scotsman, standing a little back as though he were already carrying the elements of a corporation, and his looks somewhat marred by the smallness of his eyes. Mentally, he was endowed above the average. There were but few subjects on which he could not converse with understanding and a dash of wit ; delivering himself slowly and with gusto, like a man who enjoyed his own sententiousness. He was a dry, quick, pertinent debater, speaking with a small voice, and swinging on his heels to launch and emphasise an argument. When he began a discussion, he could not bear to leave it off, but would pick the subject to the bone, without once relinquishing a point. An engineer by trade, Mackay believed in the unlimited perfectibility of all machines except the human machine. The latter he gave up with ridicule for a compound of carrion and perverse gases. He had an appetite for disconnected facts which I can only compare to

the savage taste for beads. What is called information was indeed a passion with the man, and
he not only delighted to receive it, but could pay
you back in kind.

With all these capabilities, here was Mackay,
already no longer young, on his way to a new
country, with no prospects, no money, and but
little hope. He was almost tedious in the cynical
disclosures of his despair. " The ship may go
down for me," he would say, " now or to-morrow.
I have nothing to lose and nothing to hope."
And again : " I am sick of the whole damned
performance." He was, like the kind little man
already quoted, another so-called victim of the
bottle. But Mackay was miles from publishing
his weakness to the world ; laid the blame of his
failure on corrupt masters and a corrupt State
policy ; and after he had been one night over-
taken and had played the buffoon in his cups,
sternly, though not without tact, suppressed
all reference to his escapade. It was a treat to
see him manage this ; the various jesters withered
under his gaze, and you were forced to recognise
in him a certain steely force, and a gift of command which might have ruled a senate.

In truth it was not whisky that had ruined him ;
he was ruined long before for all good human
purposes but conversation. His eyes were sealed
by a cheap, school-book materialism. He could
see nothing in the world but money and steam-
engines. He did not know what you meant by
the word happiness. He had forgotten the simple

emotions of childhood, and perhaps never encountered the delights of youth. He believed
in production, that useful figment of economy,
as if it had been real like laughter ; and production, without prejudice to liquor, was his
god and guide. One day he took me to task—
a novel cry to me—upon the over-payment of
literature. Literary men, he said, were more
highly paid than artisans ; yet the artisan made
threshing-machines and butter-churns, and the
man of letters, except in the way of a few useful
hand-books, made nothing worth the while. He
produced a mere fancy article. Mackay's notion
of a book was Hoppus's *Measurer*. Now in my
time I have possessed and even studied that
work ; but if I were to be left to-morrow on
Juan Fernandez, Hoppus's is not the book that
I should choose for my companion volume.

I tried to fight the point with Mackay. I made
him own that he had taken pleasure in reading
books otherwise, to his view, insignificant ; but
he was too wary to advance a step beyond the
admission. It was in vain for me to argue that
here was pleasure ready-made and running from
the spring, whereas his ploughs and butter-
churns were but means and mechanisms to give
men the necessary food and leisure before they
start upon the search for pleasure ; he jibbed and
ran away from such conclusions. The thing was
different, he declared, and nothing was serviceable but what had to do with food. " Eat, eat,
eat ! " he cried ; " that's the bottom and the

top." By an odd irony of circumstance, he
grew so much interested in this discussion that
he let the hour slip by unnoticed and had to go
without his tea. He had enough sense and
humour, indeed he had no lack of either, to have
chuckled over this himself in private ; and even
to me he referred to it with the shadow of a smile.

Mackay was a hot bigot. He would not hear
of religion. I have seen him waste hours of
time in argument with all sort of poor human
creatures who understood neither him nor themselves, and he had had the boyishness to dissect
and criticise even so small a matter as the riddler's
definition of mind. He snorted aloud with
zealotry and the lust for intellectual battle.
Anything, whatever it was, that seemed to him
likely to discourage the continued passionate
production of corn and steam-engines he resented
like a conspiracy against the people. Thus,
when I put in the plea for literature, that it was
only in good books, or in the society of the good,
that a man could get help in his conduct, he
declared I was in a different world from him.
" Damn my conduct ! " said he.   " I have given
it up for a bad job.   My question is, ' Can I drive
a nail ? ' "   And he plainly looked upon me as
one who was insidiously seeking to reduce the
people's annual bellyful of corn and steam-
engines.

It may be argued that these opinions spring
from the defect of culture ; that a narrow and
pinching way of life not only exaggerates to a

man the importance of material conditions, but indirectly, by denying him the necessary books and leisure, keeps his mind ignorant of larger thoughts; and that hence springs this overwhelming concern about diet, and hence the bald view of existence professed by Mackay. Had this been an English peasant the conclusion would be tenable. But Mackay had most of the elements of a liberal education. He had skirted metaphysical and mathematical studies. He had a thoughtful hold of what he knew, which would be exceptional among bankers. He had been brought up in the midst of hot-house piety, and told, with incongruous pride, the story of his own brother's deathbed ecstasies. Yet he had somehow failed to fulfil himself, and was adrift like a dead thing among external circumstances, without hope or lively preference or shaping aim. And further, there seemed a tendency among many of his fellows to fall into the same blank and unlovely opinions. One thing, indeed, is not to be learned in Scotland, and that is the way to be happy. Yet that is the whole of culture, and perhaps two-thirds of morality. Can it be that the Puritan school, by divorcing a man from nature, by thinning out his instincts, and setting a stamp of its disapproval on whole fields of human activity and interest, leads at last directly to material greed?

Nature is a good guide through life, and the love of simple pleasures next, if not superior, to virtue; and we had on board an Irishman who

based his claim to the widest and most affectionate
popularity precisely upon these two qualities,
that he was natural and happy. He boasted a
fresh colour, a tight little figure, unquenchable
gaiety, and indefatigable goodwill. His clothes
puzzled the diagnostic mind, until you heard he
had been once a private coachman, when they
became eloquent and seemed a part of his bio-
graphy. His face contained the rest, and, I
fear, a prophecy of the future ; the hawk's nose
above accorded so ill with the pink baby's mouth
below. His spirit and his pride belonged, you
might say, to the nose ; while it was the general
shiftlessness expressed by the other that had
thrown him from situation to situation, and at
length on board the emigrant ship. Barney ate,
so to speak, nothing from the galley ; his own
tea, butter and eggs supported him throughout
the voyage ; and about meal-time you might
often find him up to the elbows in amateur
cookery. His was the first voice heard singing
among all the passengers ; he was the first who
fell to dancing. From Loch Foyle to Sandy
Hook, there was not a piece of fun undertaken
but there was Barney in the midst.

You ought to have seen him when he stood up
to sing at our concerts—his tight little figure
stepping to and fro, and his feet shuffling to the
air, his eyes seeking and bestowing encouragement—and to have enjoyed the bow, so nicely
calculated between jest and earnest, between
grace and clumsiness, with which he brought

each song to a conclusion. He was not only a great favourite among ourselves, but his songs attracted the lords of the saloon, who often leaned to hear him over the rails of the hurricane-deck. He was somewhat pleased, but not at all abashed by this attention; and one night in the midst of his famous performance of " Billy Keogh," I saw him spin half round in a pirouette and throw an audacious wink to an old gentleman above.

This was the more characteristic, as, for all his daffing, he was a modest and very polite little fellow among ourselves.

He would not have hurt the feelings of a fly, nor throughout the passage did he give a shadow of offence; yet he was always, by his innocent freedoms and love of fun, brought upon that narrow margin where politeness must be natural to walk without a fall. He was once seriously angry, and that in a grave, quiet manner, because they supplied no fish on Friday; for Barney was a conscientious Catholic. He had likewise strict notions of refinement; and when, late one evening, after the women had retired, a young Scotsman struck up an indecent song, Barney's drab clothes were immediately missing from the group. His taste was for the society of gentle-men, of whom, with the reader's permission, there was no lack in our five steerages and second cabin; and he avoided the rough and positive with a girlish shrinking. Mackay, partly from his superior powers of mind, which rendered him incomprehensible, partly from his extreme opinions, was especially distasteful to the Irishman. I have seen him slink off with backward looks of terror and offended delicacy, while the other, in his witty, ugly way, had been professing hostility to God, and an extreme theatrical readiness to be shipwrecked on the spot. These utterances hurt the little coachman's modesty like a bad word.

THE SICK MAN

ONE night Jones, the young O'Reilly, and myself were walking arm-in-arm and briskly up and down the deck. Six bells had rung ; a head-wind blew chill and fitful, the fog was closing in with a sprinkle of rain, and the fog-whistle had been turned on, and now divided time with its unwelcome outcries, loud like a bull, thrilling and intense like a mosquito. Even the watch lay somewhere snugly out of sight.

For some time we observed something lying black and huddled in the scuppers, which at last heaved a little and moaned aloud. We ran to the rails. An elderly man, but whether passenger or seaman it was impossible in the darkness to determine, lay grovelling on his belly in the wet scuppers, and kicking feebly with his outspread toes. We asked him what was amiss, and he replied incoherently, with a strange accent and in a voice unmanned by terror, that he had cramp in the stomach, that he had been ailing all day, had seen the doctor twice, and had walked the deck against fatigue till he was overmastered and had fallen where we found him.

Jones remained by his side, while O'Reilly

and I hurried off to seek the doctor.   We knocked
in vain at the doctor's cabin; there came no
reply; nor could we find anyone to guide us.
It was no time for delicacy; so we ran once
more forward; and I, whipping up a ladder
and touching my hat to the officer of the watch,
addressed him as politely as I could :

" I beg your pardon, sir; but there is a man
lying bad with cramp in the lee scuppers; and
I can't find the doctor."

He looked at me peeringly in the darkness;
and then, somewhat harshly, " Well, *I* can't
leave the bridge, my man," said he.

" No, sir, but you can tell me what to do," I
returned.

" Is it one of the crew ? " he asked.

" I believe him to be a fireman," I replied.

I daresay officers are much annoyed by complaints and alarmist information from their freight
of human creatures, but certainly, whether it was
the idea that the sick man was one of the crew, or
from something conciliatory in my address, the
officer in question was immediately relieved and
mollified; and speaking in a voice much freer from
constraint, advised me to find a steward and
despatch him in quest of the doctor, who would
now be in the smoking-room over his pipe.

One of the stewards was often enough to be
found about this hour down our companion,
Steerage No. 2 and 3; that was his smoking-
room of a night. Let me call him Blackwood.
O'Reilly and I rattled down the companion,

breathing hurry; and in his short-sleeves and
perched across the carpenter's bench upon one
thigh, found Blackwood; a neat, bright, dapper,
Glasgow-looking man, with a bead of an eye and
a rank twang in his speech. I forget who was
with him, but the pair were enjoying a deliberate
talk over their pipes. I daresay he was tired
with his day's work, and eminently comfortable
at that moment; and the truth is, I did not stop
to consider his feelings, but told my story in a
breath.

" Steward," said I, " there's a man lying bad
with cramp, and I can't find the doctor."

He turned upon me as pert as a sparrow, but
with a black look that is the prerogative of man;
and taking his pipe out of his mouth—

" That's none of my business," said he. " I
don't care."

I could have strangled the little ruffian where
he sat. The thought of his cabin civility and
cabin tips filled me with indignation. I glanced
at O'Reilly; he was pale and quivering, and
looked like assault and battery, every inch of
him. But we had a better card than violence.

" You will have to make it your business," said
I, " for I am sent to you by the officer on the
bridge."

Blackwood was fairly tripped. He made no
answer, but put out his pipe, gave me one mur-
derous look, and set off upon his errand strolling.
From that day forward, I should say, he im-
proved to me in courtesy, as though he had

repented his evil speech and were anxious to leave a better impression.

When we got on deck again, Jones was still beside the sick man; and two or three late stragglers had gathered round and were offering suggestions. One proposed to give the patient water, which was promptly negatived. Another bade us hold him up; he himself prayed to be let lie; but as it was at least as well to keep him off the streaming decks, O'Reilly and I supported him between us. It was only by main force that we did so, and neither an easy nor an agreeable duty; for he fought in his paroxysms like a frightened child, and moaned miserably when he resigned himself to our control.

"O let me lie!" he pleaded. "I'll no' get better anyway." And then, with a moan that went to my heart, "O why did I come upon this miserable journey?"

I was reminded of the song which I had heard a little while before in the close, tossing steerage: "O why left I my hame?"

Meantime Jones, relieved of his immediate charge, had gone off to the galley, where he could see a light. There he found a belated cook scouring pans by the radiance of two lanterns, and one of these he sought to borrow. The scullion was backward. "Was it one of the crew?" he asked. And when Jones, smitten with my theory, had assured that it was a fireman, he reluctantly left his scouring and came towards us at an easy pace, with one of the lanterns swinging from his finger. The light, as it reached the spot, showed us an elderly man, thick-set, and grizzled with years ; but the shifting and coarse shadows concealed from us the expression and even the design of his face.

So soon as the cook set eyes on him he gave a sort of whistle.

" *It's only a passenger !* " said he ; and turning about, made, lantern and all, for the galley.

" He's a man anyway," cried Jones in indignation.

" Nobody said he was a woman," said a gruff voice, which I recognised for that of the bo's'un.

All this while there was no word of Blackwood or the doctor ; and now the officer came to our side of the ship and asked, over the hurricane-deck rails, if the doctor were not yet come. We told him not.

" No ? " he repeated with a breathing of anger ; and we saw him hurry aft in person.

Ten minutes after the doctor made his appearance deliberately enough and examined our patient with the lantern. He made little of the case, had the man brought aft to the dispensary, dosed him, and sent him forward to his bunk. Two of his neighbours in the steerage had now come to our assistance, expressing loud sorrow that such " a fine cheery body " should be sick ; and these, claiming a sort of possession, took him entirely under their own care. The drug had probably relieved him, for he struggled no more, and was led along plaintive and patient, but

protesting. His heart recoiled at the thought of
the steerage. "O let me lie down upon the
bieldy side," he cried; "O dinna take me
down!" And again: "O why did ever I come
upon this miserable voyage?" And yet once
more, with a gasp and a wailing prolongation of
the fourth word: "I had no *call* to come."
But there he was; and by the doctor's orders
and the kind force of his two shipmates dis-
appeared down the companion of Steerage No. 1
into the den allotted him.

At the foot of our own companion, just where
I had found Blackwood, Jones and the bo's'un
were now engaged in talk. This last was a gruff,
cruel-looking seaman, who must have passed
near half a century upon the seas; square-headed,
goat-bearded, with heavy blond eyebrows, and
an eye without radiance, but inflexibly steady
and hard. I had not forgotten his rough speech;
but I remembered also that he had helped us
about the lantern; and now seeing him in conversation with Jones, and being choked with
indignation, I proceeded to blow off my steam.

"Well," said I, "I make you my compliments
upon your stewards," and furiously narrated
what had happened.

"I've nothing to do with him," replied the
bo's'un. "They're all alike. They wouldn't
mind if they saw you all lying dead one upon the
top of another."

This was enough. A very little humanity
went a long way with me after the experience of

the evening. A sympathy grew up at once
between the bo's'un and myself; and that
night, and during the next few days, I learned
to appreciate him better. He was a remarkable
type, and not at all the kind of man you find in
books. He had been at Sebastopol under English
colours; and again in a States ship, " after the
Alabama, and praying God we shouldn't find
her." He was a high Tory and a high English-
man. No manufacturer could have held opinions
more hostile to the working man and his strikes.
" The workmen," he said, " think nothing of
their country. They think of nothing but themselves. They're damned greedy, selfish fellows."
He would not hear of the decadence of England.
" They say they send us beef from America,"
he argued; " but who pays for it? All the
money in the world's in England." The Royal
Navy was the best of possible services, according
to him. " Anyway the officers are gentlemen,"
said he; " and you can't get hazed to death by
a damned non-commissioned —— as you can in
the army." Among nations, England was the
first; then came France. He respected the
French navy and liked the French people; and
if he were forced to make a new choice in life,
" by God, he would try Frenchmen! " For all
his looks and rough, cold manners, I observed
that children were never frightened by him;
they divined him at once to be a friend; and one
night when he had chalked his hand and went
about stealthily setting his mark on people's

clothes, it was incongruous to hear this formidable
old salt chuckling over his boyish monkey trick.

In the morning, my first thought was of the
sick man. I was afraid I should not recognise
him, so baffling had been the light of the lantern ;
and found myself unable to decide if he were
Scots, English, or Irish. He had certainly
employed north-country words and elisions ;
but the accent and the pronunciation seemed
unfamiliar and incongruous in my ear.

To descend on an empty stomach into Steerage
No. 1, was an adventure that required some nerve.
The stench was atrocious ; each respiration
tasted in the throat like some horrible kind of
cheese ; and the squalid aspect of the place was
aggravated by so many people worming themselves into their clothes in the twilight of the
bunks. You may guess if I was pleased, not
only for him, but for myself also, when I heard
that the sick man was better and had gone on
deck.

The morning was raw and foggy, though the
sun suffused the fog with pink and amber ; the
fog-horn still blew, stertorous and intermittent ;
and to add to the discomfort, the seamen were
just beginning to wash down the decks. But
for a sick man this was heaven compared to the
steerage. I found him standing on the hot-water
pipe, just forward of the saloon deck-house. He
was smaller than I had fancied, and plain-looking ;
but his face was distinguished by strange and
fascinating eyes, limpid grey from a distance,

but, when looked into, full of changing colours
and grains of gold. His manners were mild
and uncompromisingly plain ; and I soon saw
that, when once started, he delighted to talk.
His accent and language had been formed in
the most natural way, since he was born in
Ireland, had lived a quarter of a century on the
banks of Tyne, and was married to a Scots wife.
A fisherman in the season, he had fished the east
coast from Fisherrow to Whitby. When the
season was over, and the great boats, which
required extra hands, were once drawn up on
shore till the next spring, he worked as a labourer
about chemical furnaces, or along the wharves
unloading vessels. In this comparatively humble
way of life he had gathered a competence, and
could speak of his comfortable house, his hayfield,
and his garden. On this ship, where so many
accomplished artisans were fleeing from starvation, he was present on a pleasure trip to visit a
brother in New York.

Ere he started, he informed me, he had
been warned against the steerage and the
steerage fare, and recommended to bring with
him a ham and tea and a spice loaf. But
he laughed to scorn such counsels. " *I'm*
not afraid," he had told his adviser ; " *I'll*
get on for ten days. I've not been a fisherman
for nothing." For it is no light matter, as he
reminded me, to be in an open boat, perhaps
waist-deep with herrings, day breaking with a
scowl, and for miles on every hand lee-shores,

unbroken, iron-bound, surf-beat, with only here
and there an anchorage where you dare not lie,
or a harbour impossible to enter with the wind
that blows. The life of a North Sea fisher is
one long chapter of exposure and hard work
and insufficient fare ; and even if he makes land
at some bleak fisher port, perhaps the season is
bad or his boat has been unlucky, and after fifty
hours' unsleeping vigilance and toil, not a shop
will give him credit for a loaf of bread. Yet the
steerage of the emigrant ship had been too vile
for the endurance of a man thus rudely trained.
He had scarce eaten since he came on board,
until the day before, when his appetite was
tempted by some excellent pea-soup. We were
all much of the same mind on board, and beginning with myself, had dined upon pea-soup not
wisely but too well ; only with him the excess
had been punished, perhaps because he was
weakened by former abstinence, and his first
meal had resulted in a cramp. He had determined to live henceforth on biscuit ; and when,
two months later, he should return to England,
to make the passage by saloon. The second
cabin, after due inquiry, he scouted as another
edition of the steerage.

He spoke apologetically of his emotion when
ill. " Ye see, I had no call to be here," said
he ; " and I thought it was by with me last
night. I've a good house at home, and plenty
to nurse me, and I had no real call to leave them."
Speaking of the attentions he had received from

his shipmates generally, " they were all so kind,"
he said, " that there's none to mention." And
except in so far as I might share in this,
he troubled me with no reference to my
services.

But what affected me in the most lively manner
was the wealth of this day-labourer, paying a two
months' pleasure visit to the States, and pre-
paring to return in the saloon, and the new testimony rendered by his story, not so much to the
horrors of the steerage as to the habitual comfort
of the working classes. One foggy, frosty
December evening, I encountered on Liberton
Hill, near Edinburgh, an Irish labourer trudging
homeward from the fields. Our roads lay together, and it was natural that we should fall
into talk. He was covered with mud; an in-
offensive, ignorant creature, who thought the
Atlantic Cable was a secret contrivance of the
masters the better to oppress labouring mankind; and I confess I was astonished to learn
that he had nearly three hundred pounds in the
bank. But this man had travelled over most of
the world, and enjoyed wonderful opportunities
on some American railroad, with two dollars a
shift and double pay on Sunday and at night;
whereas my fellow-passenger had never quitted
Tyneside, and had made all that he possessed in
that same accursed, down-falling England, whence
skilled mechanics, engineers, mill-wrights, and
carpenters were fleeing as from the native
country of starvation.

Fitly enough, we slid off on the subject of
strikes and wages and hard times. Being from
the Tyne, and a man who had gained and lost
in his own pocket by these fluctuations, he had
much to say, and held strong opinions on the
subject. He spoke sharply of the masters, and,
when I led him on, of the men also. The masters
had been selfish and obstructive; the men
selfish, silly, and light-headed. He rehearsed to
me the course of a meeting at which he had been
present, and the somewhat long discourse which
he had there pronounced, calling into question
the wisdom and even the good faith of the
Union delegates; and although he had escaped
himself through flush times and starvation
times with a handsomely provided purse, he had
so little faith in either man or master, and so
profound a terror for the unerring Nemesis of
mercantile affairs, that he could think of no hope
for our country outside of a sudden and complete
political subversion. Down must go Lords and
Church and Army; and capital, by some happy
direction, must change hands from worse to
better, or England stood condemned. Such
principles, he said, were growing " like a
seed."

From this mild, soft, domestic man, these words
sounded unusually ominous and grave. I had
heard enough revolutionary talk among my
workmen fellow-passengers; but most of it was
hot and turgid, and fell discredited from the lips
of unsuccessful men. This man was calm; he

had attained prosperity and ease ; he disapproved the policy which had been pursued by labour in the past ; and yet this was his panacea—to rend the old country from end to end, and from top to bottom, and in clamour and civil discord remodel it with the hand of violence.

THE STOWAWAYS

O N the Sunday, among a party of men who
were talking in our companion, Steerage
No. 2 and 3, we remarked a new figure. He wore
tweed clothes, well enough made if not very
fresh, and a plain smoking-cap. His face was
pale, with pale eyes, and spiritedly enough
designed; but though not yet thirty, a sort of
blackguardly degeneration had already over-
taken his features. The fine nose had grown
fleshy towards the point, the pale eyes were
sunk in fat. His hands were strong and elegant;
his experience of life evidently varied; his
speech full of pith and verve; his manners
forward, but perfectly presentable. The lad who
helped in the second cabin told me, in answer to
a question, that he did not know who he was, but
thought, " by his way of speaking, and because
he was so polite, that he was someone from the
saloon."

I was not so sure, for to me there was something
equivocal in his air and bearing. He might
have been, I thought, the son of some good
family who had fallen early into dissipation and
run from home. But, making every allowance,
how admirable was his talk! I wish you could
have heard him tell his own stories. They were

so swingingly set forth, in such dramatic language, and illustrated here and there by such luminous bits of acting, that they could only lose in any reproduction. There were tales of the P. and O. Company, where he had been an officer ; of the East Indies, where in former years he had lived lavishly ; of the Royal Engineers, where he had served for a period ; and of a dozen other sides of life, each introducing some vigorous thumbnail portrait. He had the talk to himself that night, we were all so glad to listen. The best talkers usually addressed themselves to some particular society ; there they are kings, elsewhere camp-followers, as a man may know Russian and yet be ignorant of Spanish ; but this fellow had a frank, headlong power of style, and a broad, human choice of subject, that would have turned any circle in the world into a circle of hearers. He was a Homeric talker, plain, strong, and cheerful ; and the things and the people of which he spoke became readily and clearly present to the minds of those who heard him. This, with a certain added colouring of rhetoric and rodomontade, must have been the style of Burns, who equally charmed the ears of duchesses and hostlers.

Yet freely and personally as he spoke, many points remained obscure in his narration. The Engineers, for instance, was a service which he praised highly ; it is true there would be trouble with the sergeants ; but then the officers were gentlemen, and his own, in particular, one among

ten thousand.   It sounded so far exactly like an
episode in the rakish, topsy-turvy life of such an
one as I had imagined.   But then there came
incidents more doubtful, which showed an almost
impudent greed after gratuities, and a truly
impudent disregard for truth.   And then there
was the tale of his departure.   He had wearied,
it seems, of Woolwich, and one fine day, with a
companion, slipped up to London for a spree.   I
have a suspicion that spree was meant to be a
long one ; but God disposes all things ; and one
morning, near Westminster Bridge, whom should
he come across but the very sergeant who had
recruited him at first !   What followed ?   He
himself indicated cavalierly that he had then
resigned.   Let us put it so.   But these resigna-
tions are sometimes very trying.

At length, after having delighted us for hours,
he took himself away from the companion ; and
I could ask Mackay who and what he was.
" That ? " said Mackay.   " Why, that's one of
the stowaways."

" No man," said the same authority, " who
has had anything to do with the sea, would ever
think of paying for a passage."   I give the
statement as Mackay's, without endorsement ;
yet I am tempted to believe that it contains a
grain of truth ; and if you add that the man
should be impudent and thievish, or else dead-
broke, it may even pass for a fair representation
of the facts.   We gentlemen of England who live
at home at ease have, I suspect, very insufficient

idea on the subject. All the world over, people
are stowing away in coal-holes and dark corners,
and when ships are once out to sea, appearing
again, begrimed and bashful, upon deck. The
career of these sea-tramps partakes largely of
the adventurous. They may be poisoned by
coal-gas, or die by starvation in their place of
concealment ; or when found they may be
clapped at once and ignominiously into irons,
thus to be carried to their promised land, the
port of destination, and alas ! brought back in
the same way to that from which they started,
and there delivered over to the magistrates and
the seclusion of a county jail. Since I crossed
the Atlantic, one miserable stowaway was found
in a dying state among the fuel, uttered but a
word or two, and departed for a farther country
than America.

When the stowaway appears on deck, he had
but one thing to pray for : that he be set to work,
which is the price and sign of his forgiveness.
After half an hour with a swab or a bucket, he
feels himself as secure as if he had paid for his
passage. It is not altogether a bad thing for
the company, who get more or less efficient hands
for nothing but a few plates of junk and duff ;
and every now and again find themselves better
paid than by a whole family of cabin passengers.
Not long ago, for instance, a packet was saved
from nearly certain loss by the skill and courage
of a stowaway engineer. As was no more than
just, a handsome subscription rewarded him for

his success ; but even without such exceptional good fortune, as things stand in England and America, the stowaway will often make a good profit out of his adventure. Four engineers stowed away last summer on the same ship, the *Circassia ;* and before two days after their arrival each of the four had found a comfortable berth. This was the most hopeful tale of emigration that I heard from first to last ; and as you see, the luck was for stowaways.

My curiosity was much inflamed by what I heard ; and the next morning, as I was making the round of the ship, I was delighted to find the ex-Royal Engineer engaged in washing down the white paint of a deck-house. There was another fellow at work beside him, a lad not more than twenty, in the most miraculous tatters, his handsome face sown with grains of beauty and lighted up by expressive eyes. Four stowaways had been found aboard our ship before she left the Clyde, but these two had alone escaped the ignominy of being put ashore. Alick, my acquaintance of last night, was Scots by birth, and by trade a practical engineer ; the other was from Devonshire, and had been to sea before the mast. Two people more unlike by training, character, and habits, it would be hard to imagine ; yet here they were together, scrubbing paint.

Alick had held all sorts of good situations, and wasted many opportunities in life. I have heard him end a story with these words : " That was

in my golden days, when I used finger-glasses."
Situation after situation failed him; then followed the depression of trade, and for months he
had hung round with other idlers, playing marbles
all day in the West Park, and going home at
night to tell his landlady how he had been seeking
for a job. I believe this kind of existence was
not unpleasant to Alick himself, and he might
have long continued to enjoy idleness and a life
on tick; but he had a comrade, let us call him
Brown, who grew restive. This fellow was continually threatening to slip his cable for the
States, and at last, one Wednesday, Glasgow
was left widowed of her Brown. Some months
afterwards, Alick met another old chum in
Sauchiehall Street.

"By the by, Alick," said he, "I met a
gentleman in New York who was asking for
you."

"Who was that?" asked Alick.

"The second engineer on board the *So-and-so*,"
was the reply.

"Well, and who is he?"

"Brown, to be sure."

For Brown had been one of the fortunate
quartette aboard the *Circassia*. If that was the
way of it in the States, Alick thought it was
high time to follow Brown's example. He spent
his last day, as he put it, "reviewing the yeo-
manry," and the next morning says he to his
landlady, "Mrs. X, I'll not take porridge to-day,
please; I'll take some eggs."

" Why, have you found a job ? " she asked,
delighted.

" Well, yes," returned the perfidious Alick ;
" I think I'll start to-day."

And so, well lined with eggs, start he did, but
for America. I am afraid that landlady has seen
the last of him.

It was easy enough to get on board in the confusion that attends a vessel's departure ; and in
one of the dark corners of Steerage No. 1, flat in
a bunk and with an empty stomach, Alick made
the voyage from the Broomielaw to Greenock.
That night, the ship's yeoman pulled him out
by the heels and had him before the mate. Two
other stowaways had already been found and
sent ashore ; but by this time darkness had fallen,
they were out in the middle of the estuary, and
the last steamer had left them till the morning.
" Take him to the forecastle and give him a
meal," said the mate, " and see and pack him off
the first thing to-morrow."

In the forecastle he had supper, a good night's
rest, and breakfast ; and was sitting placidly
with a pipe, fancying all was over and the game
up for good with that ship, when one of the
sailors grumbled out an oath at him, with a
" What are you doing there ?" and " Do you call
that hiding, anyway ? " There was need of no
more ; Alick was in another bunk before the day
was older. Shortly before the passengers arrived,
the ship was cursorily inspected. He heard the
round come down the companion and look into

one pen after another, until they came within two of the one in which he lay concealed. Into these last two they did not enter, but merely glanced from without; and Alick had no doubt that he was personally favoured in this escape. It was the character of the man to attribute nothing to luck and but little to kindness; whatever happened to him he had earned in his own right amply; favours came to him from his singular attraction and adroitness, and misfortunes he had always accepted with his eyes open. Half an hour after the searchers had departed, the steerage began to fill with legitimate passengers, and the worst of Alick's troubles was at an end. He was soon making himself popular, smoking other people's tobacco and politely sharing their private stock of delicacies, and when night came he retired to his bunk beside the others with composure.

Next day by afternoon, Lough Foyle being already far behind, and only the rough northwestern hills of Ireland within view, Alick appeared on deck to court inquiry and decide his fate. As a matter of fact, he was known to several on board, and even intimate with one of the engineers; but it was plainly not the etiquette of such occasions for the authorities to avow their information. Every one professed surprise and anger on his appearance, and he was led prisoner before the captain.

" What have you got to say for yourself ? " inquired the captain.

" Not much," said Alick ; " but when a man
has been a long time out of a job, he will do
things he would not under other circumstances."

" Are you willing to work ? "

Alick swore he was burning to be useful.

" And what can you do ? " asked the captain.

He replied composedly that he was a brass-
fitter by trade.

" I think you will be better at engineering ? "
suggested the officer, with a shrewd look.

" No, sir," said Alick simply.—" There's few
can beat me at a lie," was his engaging commen-
tary to me as he recounted the affair.

" Have you been to sea ? " again asked the
captain.

" I've had a trip on a Clyde steamboat, sir,
but no more," replied the unabashed Alick.

" Well, we must try and find some work for
you," concluded the officer.

And hence we behold Alick, clear of the hot
engine-room, lazily scraping paint and now and
then taking a pull upon a sheet. " You leave
me alone," was his deduction. " When I get
talking to a man, I can get round him."

The other stowaway, whom I will call the
Devonian—it was noticeable that neither of them
told his name—had both been brought up and
seen the world in a much smaller way. His
father, a confectioner, died and was closely
followed by his mother. His sisters had taken,
I think, to dressmaking. He himself had returned from sea about a year ago and gone to

live with his brother, who kept the " George Hotel "—" it was not quite a real hotel," added the candid fellow—" and had a hired man to mind the horses." At first the Devonian was very welcome ; but as time went on his brother not unnaturally grew cool towards him, and he began to find himself one too many at the " George Hotel." " I don't think brothers care much for you," he said, as a general reflection upon life. Hurt at this change, nearly penniless, and too proud to ask for more, he set off on foot and walked eighty miles to Weymouth, living on the journey as he could. He would have enlisted, but he was too small for the army and too old for the navy ; and thought himself fortunate at last to find a berth on board a trading dandy. Somewhere in the Bristol Channel, the dandy sprung a leak and went down ; and though the crew were picked up and brought ashore by fishermen, they found themselves with nothing but the clothes upon their back. His next engagement was scarcely better starred ; for the ship proved so leaky, and frightened them all so heartily during a short passage through the Irish Sea, that the entire crew deserted and remained behind upon the quays of Belfast.

Evil days were now coming thick on the Devonian. He could find no berth in Belfast, and had to work a passage to Glasgow on a steamer. She reached the Broomielaw on a Wednesday : the Devonian had a bellyful that morning, laying in breakfast manfully to provide

against the future, and set off along the quays
to seek employment.   But he was now not only
penniless, his clothes had begun to fall in tatters ;
he had begun to have the look of a street Arab ;
and captains will have nothing to say to a raga-
muffin ; for in that trade, as in all others, it is
the coat that depicts the man.   You may hand,
reef, and steer like an angel, but if you have a
hole in your trousers, it is like a millstone round
your neck.   The Devonian lost heart at so many
refusals.   He had not the impudence to beg ;
although, as he said, "when I had money of
my own, I always gave it."   It was only on
Saturday morning, after three whole days of
starvation, that he asked a scone from a milk-
woman, who added of her own accord a glass
of milk.   He had now made up his mind to stow
away, not from any desire to see America, but
merely to obtain the comfort of a place in the
forecastle and a supply of familiar sea-fare.   He
lived by begging, always from milkwomen, and
always scones and milk, and was not once refused.
It was vile wet weather, and he could never have
been dry.   By night he walked the streets, and
by day slept upon Glasgow Green, and heard, in
the intervals of his dozing, the famous theologians
of the spot clear up intricate points of doctrine
and appraise the merits of the clergy.   He had
not much instruction ; he could "read bills on
the street," but was "main bad at writing " ;
yet these theologians seem to have impressed him
with a genuine sense of amusement.   Why he did

not go to the Sailor's Home I know not; I
presume there is in Glasgow one of these insti-
tutions, which are by far the happiest and the
wisest effort of contemporaneous charity; but
I must stand to my author, as they say in old
books, and relate the story as I heard it. In the
meantime, he had tried four times to stow away
in different vessels, and four times had been discovered and handed back to starvation. The
fifth time was lucky; and you may judge if he were
pleased to be aboard ship again, at his old work,
and with duff twice a week. He was, said Alick,
" a devil for the duff." Or if devil was not the
word, it was one if anything stronger.

The difference in the conduct of the two was
remarkable. The Devonian was as willing as
any paid hand, swarmed aloft among the first,
pulled his natural weight and firmly upon a
rope, and found work for himself when there
was none to show him. Alick, on the other hand,
was not only a skulker in the grain, but took a
humorous and fine gentlemanly view of the
transaction. He would speak to me by the hour
in ostentatious idleness; and only if the bo's'un
or a mate came by, fell-to languidly for just the
necessary time till they were out of sight. " I'm
not breaking my heart with it," he remarked.

Once there was a hatch to be opened near
where he was stationed; he watched the prepara-
tions for a second or so suspiciously, and then,
" Hullo," said he, " here's some real work
coming—I'm off," and he was gone that moment,

Again, calculating the six guinea passage-money, and the probable duration of the passage, he remarked pleasantly that he was getting six shillings a day for this job, " and it's pretty dear to the company at that." " They are making nothing by me," was another of his observations ; " they're making something by that fellow." And he pointed to the Devonian, who was just then busy to the eyes.

The more you saw of Alick, the more, it must be owned, you learned to despise him. His natural talents were of no use either to himself or others ; for his character had degenerated like his face, and become pulpy and pretentious. Even his power of persuasion, which was certainly very surprising, stood in some danger of being lost or neutralised by over-confidence. He lied in an aggressive, brazen manner, like a pert criminal in the dock ; and he was so vain of his own cleverness that he could not refrain from boasting, ten minutes after, of the very trick by which he had deceived you. " Why, now I have more money than when I came on board," he said one night, exhibiting a sixpence, " and yet I stood myself a bottle of beer before I went to bed yesterday. And as for tobacco, I have fifteen sticks of it." That was fairly successful indeed ; yet a man of his superiority, and with a less obtrusive policy, might, who knows ? have got the length of half a crown. A man who prides himself upon persuasion should learn the persuasive faculty of silence, above all as to his own misdeeds. It is only in the farce and for dramatic purposes that Scapin enlarges on his peculiar talents to the world at large.

Scapin is perhaps a good name for this clever, unfortunate Alick; for at the bottom of all his misconduct there was a guiding sense of humour that moved you to forgive him. It was more than half a jest that he conducted his existence. " Oh, man," he said to me once with unusual emotion, like a man thinking of his mistress, " I would give up anything for a lark."

It was in relation to his fellow-stowaway that Alick showed the best, or perhaps I should say, the only, good points of his nature. " Mind you," he said suddenly, changing his tone, " mind you that's a good boy. He wouldn't tell you a lie. A lot of them think he is a scamp because his clothes are ragged, but he isn't; he's as good as gold." To hear him, you became aware that Alick himself had a taste for virtue. He thought his own idleness and the other's industry equally becoming. He was no more anxious to insure his own reputation as a liar than to uphold the truthfulness of his companion; and he seemed unaware of what was incongruous in his attitude, and was plainly sincere in both characters.

It was not surprising that he should take an interest in the Devonian, for the lad worshipped and served him in love and wonder. Busy as he was, he would find time to warn Alick of an approaching officer, or even to tell him that the

coast was clear, and he might slip off and smoke
a pipe in safety. "Tom," he once said to him,
for that was the name which Alick ordered him
to use, "if you don't like going to the galley,
I'll go for you. You ain't used to this kind of
thing, you ain't. But I'm a sailor ; and I can
understand the feelings of any fellow, I can."
Again, he was hard up, and casting about for
some tobacco, for he was not so liberally used
in this respect as others perhaps less worthy,
when Alick offered him the half of one of his
fifteen sticks. I think, for my part, he might
have increased the offer to a whole one, or
perhaps a pair of them, and not lived to regret
his liberality. But the Devonian refused. "No,"
he said, "you're a stowaway like me ; I won't
take it from you, I'll take it from someone who's
not down on his luck."

It was notable in this generous lad that he
was strongly under the influence of sex If a
woman passed near where he was working, his
eyes lit up, his hand paused, and his mind
wandered instantly to other thoughts. It was
natural that he should exercise a fascination
proportionately strong upon women. He begged,
you will remember, from women only, and was
never refused. Without wishing to explain away
the charity of those who helped him, I cannot
but fancy he may have owed a little to his handsome face, and to that quick, responsive nature,
formed for love, which speaks eloquently through
all disguises, and can stamp an impression in

ten minutes' talk or an exchange of glances.
He was the more dangerous in that he was far
from bold, but seemed to woo in spite of himself,
and with a soft and pleading eye. Ragged as he
was, and many a scarecrow is in that respect
more comfortably furnished, even on board he
was not without some curious admirers.

There was a girl among the passengers, a tall,
blonde, handsome, strapping Irishwoman, with a
wild, accommodating eye, whom Alick had dubbed
Tommy, with that transcendental appropriate-
ness that defies analysis. One day the Devonian
was lying for warmth in the upper stoke-hole,
which stands open on the deck, when Irish Tommy
came past, very neatly attired, as was her custom.

" Poor fellow," she said, stopping, " you
haven't a vest."

" No," he said ; " I wish I 'ad."

Then she stood and gazed on him in silence,
until, in his embarrassment, for he knew not how
to look under this scrutiny, he pulled out his
pipe and began to fill it with tobacco.

" Do you want a match ? " she asked. And
before he had time to reply, she ran off and
presently returned with more than one.

That was the beginning and the end, as far as
our passage is concerned, of what I will make
bold to call this love-affair. There are many
relations which go on to marriage and last during
a lifetime, in which less human feeling is engaged
than in this scene of five minutes at the stoke-
hole.

Rigidly speaking, this would end the chapter of the stowaways ; but in a larger sense of the word I have yet more to add. Jones had discovered and pointed out to me a young woman who was remarkable among her fellows for a pleasing and interesting air. She was poorly clad, to the verge, if not over the line, of disrespectability, with a ragged old jacket and a bit of a sealskin cap no bigger than your fist ; but her eyes, her whole expression, and her manner, even in ordinary moments, told of a true womanly nature, capable of love, anger, and devotion. She had a look, too, of refinement, like one who might have been a better lady than most, had she been allowed the opportunity. When alone she seemed pre-occupied and sad ; but she was not often alone ; there was usually by her side a heavy, dull, gross man in rough clothes, chary of speech and gesture—not from caution, but poverty of disposition ; a man like a ditcher, unlovely and uninteresting ; whom she petted and tended and waited on with her eyes as if he had been Amadis of Gaul. It was strange to see this hulking fellow dog-sick, and this delicate, sad woman caring for him. He seemed, from first to last, insensible of her caresses and attentions, and she seemed unconscious of his insensibility. The Irish husband, who sang his wife to sleep, and this Scottish girl serving her Orson, were the two bits of human nature that most appealed to me throughout the voyage.

On the Thursday before we arrived, the tickets

were collected; and soon a rumour began to go round the vessel; and this girl, with her bit of sealskin cap, became the centre of whispering and pointed fingers. She also, it was said, was a stowaway of a sort; for she was on board with neither ticket nor money; and the man with whom she travelled was the father of a family, who had left wife and children to be hers. The ship's officers discouraged the story, which may therefore have been a story and no more; but it was believed in the steerage, and the poor girl had to encounter many curious eyes from that day forth.

PERSONAL EXPERIENCE AND REVIEW

TRAVEL is of two kinds; and this voyage of mine across the ocean combined both. " Out of my country and myself I go," sings the old poet; and I was not only travelling out of my country in latitude and longitude, but out of myself in diet, associates, and consideration. Part of the interest and a great deal of the amusement flowed, at least to me, from this novel situation in the world.

I found that I had what they call fallen in life with absolute success and verisimilitude. I was taken for a steerage passenger; no one seemed surprised that I should be so; and there was nothing but the brass plate between decks to remind me that I had once been a gentleman. In a former book, describing a former journey, I expressed some wonder that I could be readily and naturally taken for a pedlar, and explained the accident by the difference of language and manners between England and France. I must now take a humbler view; for here I was among my own countrymen, somewhat roughly clad, to be sure, but with every advantage of speech and manner; and I am bound to confess that I passed for nearly anything you please except an educated gentleman. The sailors called me

" mate," the officers addressed me as " my man," my comrades accepted me without hesitation for a person of their own character and experience, but with some curious information. One, a mason himself, believed I was a mason ; several, and among these at least one of the seamen, judged me to be a petty officer in the American navy ; and I was so often set down for a practical engineer that at last I had not the heart to deny it. From all these guesses I drew one conclusion, which told against the insight of my companions. They might be close observers in their own way, and read the manners in the face ; but it was plain that they did not extend their observation to the hands.

To the saloon passengers also I sustained my part without a hitch. It is true I came little in their way ; but when we did encounter, there was no recognition in their eye, although I confess I sometimes courted it in silence. All these, my inferiors and equals, took me, like the transformed monarch in the story, for a mere common, human man. They gave me a hard, dead look, with the flesh about the eye kept unrelaxed.

With the women this surprised me less, as I had already experimented on the sex by going abroad through a suburban part of London simply attired in a sleeve-waistcoat. The result was curious. I then learned for the first time, and by the exhaustive process, how much attention ladies are accustomed to bestow on all male creatures of their own station ; for, in my humble rig, each one who went by me caused me a certain shock of surprise and a sense of something wanting. In my normal circumstances, it appeared every young lady must have paid me some tribute of a glance; and though I had often not detected it when it was given, I was well aware of its absence when it was withheld. My height seemed to decrease with every woman who passed me, for she passed me like a dog. This is one of my grounds for supposing that what are called the upper classes may sometimes produce a disagreeable impression in what are called the lower; and I wish someone would continue my experiment, and find out exactly at what stage of toilette a man becomes invisible to the well-regulated female eye.

Here on shipboard the matter was put to a more complete test; for, even with the addition of speech and manner, I passed among the ladies for precisely the average man of the steerage. It was one afternoon that I saw this demonstrated. A very plainly dressed woman was taken ill on deck. I think I had the luck to be present at every sudden seizure during all the passage; and on this occasion found myself in the place of importance, supporting the sufferer. There was not only a large crowd immediately around us, but a considerable knot of saloon passengers leaning over our heads from the hurricane-deck. One of these, an elderly managing woman, hailed me with counsels. Of course I had to reply; and as the talk went on, I began to discover that

the whole group took me for the husband. I
looked upon my new wife, poor creature, with
mingled feelings ; and I must own she had not
even the appearance of the poorest class of city
servant-maids, but looked more like a country
wench, who should have been employed at a
roadside inn. Now was the time for me to go
and study the brass plate.

To such of the officers as knew about me—the
doctor, the purser, and the stewards—I appeared
in the light of a broad joke. The fact that I
spent the better part of my day in writing had
gone abroad over the ship and tickled them all
prodigiously. Whenever they met me they
referred to my absurd occupation with familiarity
and breadth of humorous intention. Their
manner was well calculated to remind me of
my fallen fortunes. You may be sincerely
amused by the amateur literary efforts of a
gentleman, but you scarce publish the feeling to
his face. " Well ! " they would say : " still
writing ? " And the smile would widen into a
laugh. The purser came one day into the cabin,
and, touched to the heart by my misguided
industry, offered me some other kind of writing,
" for which," he added pointedly, " you will be
paid." This was nothing else than to copy out
the list of passengers.

Another trick of mine which told against my
reputation was my choice of roosting-place in an
active draught upon the cabin floor. I was
openly jeered and flouted for this eccentricity ;

and a considerable knot would sometimes gather
at the door to see my last dispositions for the
night. This was embarrassing, but I learned to
support the trial with equanimity.

Indeed, I may say that, upon the whole, my
new position sat lightly and naturally upon my
spirits. I accepted the consequences with readiness, and found them far from difficult to bear.
The steerage conquered me ; I conformed more
and more to the type of the place, not only in
manner but at heart, growing hostile to the
officers and cabin passengers who looked down
upon me, and day by day greedier for small
delicacies. Such was the result, as I fancy, of
a diet of bread and butter, soup and porridge.
We think we have no sweet tooth as long as we
are full to the brim of molasses ; but a man must
have sojourned in the workhouse before he boasts
himself indifferent to dainties. Every evening,
for instance, I was more and more pre-occupied
about our doubtful fare at tea. If it was delicate
my heart was much lightened ; if it was but
broken fish I was proportionally downcast.
The offer of a little jelly from a fellow-passenger
more provident than myself caused a marked
elevation in my spirits. And I would have gone
to the ship's end and back again for an oyster
or a chipped fruit.

In other ways I was content with my position.
It seemed no disgrace to be confounded with
my company ; for I may as well declare at once
I found their manners as gentle and becoming as

those of any other class.   I do not mean that my
friends could have sat down without embarrassment and laughable disaster at the table of a
duke.   That does not imply an inferiority of
breeding, but a difference of usage.   Thus I
flatter myself that I conducted myself well among
my fellow-passengers ;   yet my most ambitious
hope is not to have avoided faults, but to have
committed as few as possible.   I know too well
that my tact is not the same as their tact, and
that my habit of a different society constituted,
not only no qualification, but a positive dis-
ability to move easily and becomingly in this.
When Jones complimented me—because I " managed to behave very pleasantly " to my fellow-
passengers, was how he put it—I could follow
the thought in his mind, and knew his compli-
ment to be such as we pay foreigners on their
proficiency in English.   I dare say this praise
was given me immediately on the back of some
unpardonable solecism, which had led him to
review my conduct as a whole.   We are all ready
to laugh at the ploughman among lords ;   we
should consider also the case of a lord among the
ploughmen.   I have seen a lawyer in the house
of a Hebridean fisherman ;   and I know, but
nothing will induce me to disclose, which of
these two was the better gentleman.   Some of
our finest behaviour, though it looks well enough
from the boxes, may seem even brutal to the
gallery.   We boast too often manners that are
parochial rather than universal ;   that, like a

country wine, will not bear transportation for a
hundred miles, nor from the parlour to the kitchen.
To be a gentleman is to be one all the world
over, and in every relation and grade of society.
It is a high calling, to which a man must first
be born, and then devote himself for life.   And,
unhappily, the manners of a certain so-called
upper grade have a kind of currency, and meet
with a certain external acceptation throughout
all the others, and this tends to keep us well
satisfied with slight acquirements and the
amateurish accomplishments of a clique.   But
manners, like art, should be human and central.

Some of my fellow-passengers, as I now moved
among them in a relation of equality, seemed to
me excellent gentlemen.   They were not rough,
nor hasty, nor disputatious ; debated pleasantly,
differed kindly ; were helpful, gentle, patient,
and placid.   The type of manners was plain, and
even heavy ; there was little to please the eye,
but nothing to shock ; and I thought gentleness
lay more nearly at the spring of behaviour than in
many more ornate and delicate societies.   I say
delicate, where I cannot say refined ; a thing
may be fine like ironwork, without being delicate
like lace.   There was here less delicacy ; the
skin supported more callously the natural surface
of events, the mind received more bravely the
crude facts of human existence ; but I do not
think that there was less effective refinement,
less consideration for others, less polite suppres-
sion of self.   I speak of the best among my

fellow-passengers; for in the steerage, as well as in the saloon, there is a mixture. Those, then, with whom I found myself in sympathy, and of whom I may therefore hope to write with a greater measure of truth, were not only as good in their manners, but endowed with very much the same natural capacities, and about as wise in deduction, as the bankers and barristers of what is called society. One and all were too much interested in disconnected facts, and loved information for its own sake with too rash a devotion; but people in all classes display the same appetite as they gorge themselves daily with the miscellaneous gossip of the newspaper. Newspaper reading, as far as I can make out, is often rather a sort of brown study than an act of culture. I have myself palmed off yesterday's issue on a friend, and seen him re-peruse it for a continuance of minutes with an air at once refreshed and solemn. Workmen, perhaps, pay more attention; but though they may be eager listeners, they have rarely seemed to me either willing or careful thinkers. Culture is not measured by the greatness of the field which is covered by our knowledge, but by the nicety with which we can perceive relations in that field, whether great or small. Workmen, certainly those who were on board with me, I found wanting in this quality or habit of the mind. They did not perceive relations, but leaped to a so-called cause, and thought the problem settled. Thus the cause of everything in England was the

form of government, and the cure for all
evils was, by consequence, a revolution. It is
surprising how many of them said this, and that
none should have had a definite thought in his head
as he said it. Some hated the Church because
they disagreed with it ; some hated Lord Beacons-
field because of war and taxes ; all hated the
masters, possibly with reason. But these feelings were not at the root of the matter ; the
true reasoning of their souls ran thus—I have not
got on ; I ought to have got on ; if there was a
revolution I should get on. How ? They had
no idea. Why ? Because—because—well, look
at America !

To be politically blind is no distinction ; we
are all so, if you come to that. At bottom, as it
seems to me, there is but one question in modern
home politics, though it appears in many shapes,
and that is the question of money ; and but one
political remedy, that the people should grow
wiser and better. My workmen fellow-passengers
were as impatient and dull of hearing on the
second of these points as any member of Parlia-
ment ; but they had some glimmerings of the
first. They would not hear of improvement on
their part, but wished the world made over again
in a crack, so that they might remain improvident
and idle and debauched, and yet enjoy the comfort and respect that should accompany the
opposite virtues ; and it was in this expectation,
as far as I could see, that many of them were
now on their way to America. But on the point

of money they saw clearly enough that inland politics, so far as they were concerned, were reducible to the question of annual income ; a question which should long ago have been settled by a revolution, they did not know how, and which they were now about to settle for themselves, once more they knew not how, by crossing the Atlantic in a steamship of considerable tonnage.

And yet it has been amply shown them that the second or income question is in itself nothing, and may as well be left undecided, if there be no wisdom and virtue to profit by the change. It is not by a man's purse, but by his character, that he is rich or poor. Barney will be poor, Alick will be poor, Mackay will be poor ; let them go where they will, and wreck all the governments under heaven, they will be poor until they die.

Nothing is perhaps more notable in the average workman than his surprising idleness, and the candour with which he confesses to the failing. It has to me been always something of a relief to find the poor, as a general rule, so little oppressed with work. I can in consequence enjoy my own more fortunate beginning with a better grace. The other day I was living with a farmer in America, an old frontiersman, who had worked and fought, hunted and farmed, from his childhood up. He excused himself for his defective education on the ground that he had been overworked from first to last. Even now, he said,

anxious as he was, he had never the time to take
up a book. In consequence of this, I observed
him closely ; he was occupied for four or, at the
extreme outside, for five hours out of the twenty-
four, and then principally in walking ; and the
remainder of the day he passed in born idleness,
either eating fruit or standing with his back
against a door. I have known men do hard
literary work all morning, and then undergo
quite as much physical fatigue by way of relief
as satisfied this powerful frontiersman for the
day. He, at least, like all the educated class, did
so much homage to industry as to persuade himself he was industrious. But the average mechanic
recognises his idleness with effrontery ; he has
even, as I am told, organised it.

I give the story as it was told me, and it was
told me for a fact. A man fell from a housetop
in the city of Aberdeen, and was brought into
hospital with broken bones. He was asked what
was his trade, and replied that he was a *tapper*.
No one had ever heard of such a thing before ;
the officials were filled with curiosity ; they
besought an explanation. It appeared that when
a party of slaters were engaged upon a roof, they
would now and then be taken with a fancy for
the public-house. Now a seamstress, for example,
might slip away from her work and no one be
the wiser ; but if these fellows adjourned, the
tapping of the mallets would cease, and thus the
neighbourhood be advertised of their defection.
Hence the career of the tapper. He has to do

the tapping and keep up an industrious bustle on the housetop during the absence of the slaters. When he taps for only one or two the thing is child's-play, but when he has to represent a whole troop, it is then that he earns his money in the sweat of his brow. Then must he bound from spot to spot, reduplicate, triplicate, sex-duplicate his single personality, and swell and hasten his blows, until he produce a perfect illusion for the ear, and you would swear that a crowd of emulous masons were continuing merrily to roof the house. It must be a strange sight from an upper window.

I heard nothing on board of the tapper; but I was astonished at the stories told by my companions. Skulking, shirking, malingering, were all established tactics, it appeared. They could see no dishonesty where a man who is paid for an hour's work gives half an hour's consistent idling in its place. Thus the tapper would refuse to watch for the police during a burglary, and call himself an honest man. It is not sufficiently recognised that our race detests to work. If I thought that I should have to work every day of my life as hard as I am working now, I should be tempted to give up the struggle. And the workman early begins on his career of toil. He has never had his fill of holidays in the past, and his prospect of holidays in the future is both distant and uncertain. In the circumstances, it would require a high degree of virtue not to snatch alleviations for the moment.

There were many good talkers on the ship;
and I believe good talking of a certain sort is a
common accomplishment among working men.
Where books are comparatively scarce, a greater
amount of information will be given and received
by word of mouth; and this tends to produce
good talkers, and, what is no less needful for
conversation, good listeners. They could all tell
a story with effect. I am sometimes tempted
to think that the less literary class show always
better in narration; they have so much more
patience with detail, are so much less hurried to
reach the points, and preserve so much juster
a proportion among the facts. At the same time
their talk is dry; they pursue a topic ploddingly,
have not an agile fancy, do not throw sudden
lights from unexpected quarters, and when the
talk is over they often leave the matter where it
was. They mark time instead of marching.
They think only to argue, not to reach new conclusions, and use their reason rather as a weapon
of offence than as a tool for self-improvement.
Hence the talk of some of the cleverest was
unprofitable in result, because there was no give
and take; they would grant you as little as
possible for premise, and begin to dispute under
an oath to conquer or to die.

But the talk of a workman is apt to be more
interesting than that of a wealthy merchant,
because the thoughts, hopes, and fears of which
the workman's life is built lie nearer to necessity
and nature. They are more immediate to human

life. An income calculated by the week is a far more human thing than one calculated by the year, and a small income, simply from its smallness, than a large one. I never wearied listening to the details of a workman's economy, because every item stood for some real pleasure. If he could afford pudding twice a week, you know that twice a week the man ate with genuine gusto and was physically happy; while if you learn that a rich man has seven courses a day, ten to one the half of them remain untasted, and the whole is but misspent money and a weariness to the flesh.

The difference between England and America to a working man was thus most humanly put to me by a fellow-passenger: " In America," said he, " you get pies and puddings." I do not hear enough, in economy books, of pies and pudding. A man lives in and for the delicacies, adornments, and accidental attributes of life, such as pudding to eat and pleasant books and theatres to occupy his leisure. The bare terms of existence would be rejected with contempt by all. If a man feeds on bread and butter, soup and porridge, his appetite grows wolfish after dainties. And the workman dwells in a borderland, and is always within sight of those cheerless regions where life is more difficult to sustain than worth sustaining. Every detail of our existence, where it is worth while to cross the ocean after pie and pudding, is made alive and enthralling by the presence of genuine desire; but it is all one to

me whether Crœsus has a hundred or a thousand
thousands in the bank.   There is more adventure
in the life of the working man who descends as
a common soldier into the battle of life, than in
that of the millionaire who sits apart in an office,
like Von Moltke, and only directs the manœuvres
by telegraph.   Give me to hear about the career
of him who is in the thick of the business ; to
whom one change of market means an empty
belly, and another a copious and savoury meal.
This is not the philosophical, but the human side
of economics ; it interests like a story ; and the
life of all who are thus situated partakes in a small
way of the charm of *Robinson Crusoe ;* for every
step is critical, and human life is presented to
you naked and verging to its lowest terms.

NEW YORK

A S we drew near to New York I was at first
amused, and then somewhat staggered, by
the cautious and grisly tales that went the round.
You would have thought we were to land upon a
cannibal island. You must speak to no one in
the streets, as they would not leave you till you
were rooked and beaten. You must enter a
hotel with military precautions; for the least
you had to apprehend was to awake next morning without money or baggage, or necessary
raiment, a lone forked radish in a bed; and if
the worst befell, you would instantly and
mysteriously disappear from the ranks of mankind.
I have usually found such stories correspond
to the least modicum of fact. Thus I was warned,
I remember, against the roadside inns of the
Cevennes, and that by a learned professor; and
when I reached Pradelles the warning was explained; it was but the far-away rumour and
reduplication of a single terrifying story already
half a century old, and half forgotten in the
theatre of the events. So I was tempted to
make light of these reports against America.
But we had on board with us a man whose
evidence it would not do to put aside. He had
come near these perils in the body; he had

visited a robber inn. The public has an old and
well-grounded favour for this class of incident,
and shall be gratified to the best of my power.

My fellow-passenger, whom we shall call
M'Naughten, had come from New York to Boston
with a comrade, seeking work. They were a
pair of rattling blades; and, leaving their
baggage at the station, passed the day in beer-
saloons, and with congenial spirits, until midnight
struck. Then they applied themselves to find a
lodging, and walked the streets till two, knocking
at houses of entertainment and being refused
admittance, or themselves declining the terms.
By two the inspiration of their liquor had begun
to wear off; they were weary and humble, and
after a great circuit found themselves in the same
street where they had begun their search, and in
front of a French hotel where they had already
sought accommodation. Seeing the house still
open, they returned to the charge. A man in a
white cap sat in an office by the door. He
seemed to welcome them more warmly than
when they had first presented themselves, and
the charge for the night had somewhat unaccount-
ably fallen from a dollar to a quarter. They
thought him ill-looking, but paid their quarter
apiece, and were shown upstairs to the top of
the house. There, in a small room, the man in
the white cap wished them pleasant slumbers.

It was furnished with a bed, a chair, and some
conveniences. The door did not lock on the
inside; and the only sign of adornment was a

couple of framed pictures, one close above the
head of the bed, and the other opposite the foot,
and both curtained, as we may sometimes see
valuable water-colours, or the portraits of the
dead, or works of art more than usually skittish
in the subject. It was perhaps in the hope of
finding something of this last description that
M'Naughten's comrade pulled aside the curtain
of the first. He was startingly disappointed.
There was no picture. The frame surrounded,
and the curtain was designed to hide, an oblong
aperture in the partition, through which they
looked forth into the dark corridor. A person
standing without could easily take a purse from
under the pillow, or even strangle a sleeper as
he lay abed. M'Naughten and his comrade
stared at each other like Balboa and his men,
" with a wild surmise " ; and then the latter,
catching up the lamp, ran to the other frame
and roughly raised the curtain. There he stood,
petrified ; and M'Naughten, who had followed,
grasped him by the wrist in terror. They could
see into another room, larger in size than that
which they occupied, where three men sat
crouching and silent in the dark. For a second
or so these five persons looked each other in
the eyes, then the curtain was dropped, and
M'Naughten and his friend made but one bolt
of it out of the room and downstairs. The man
in the white cap said nothing as they passed
him ; and they were so pleased to be once more
in the open night that they gave up all notion

of a bed, and walked the streets of Boston till the morning.

No one seemed much cast down by these stories, but all inquired after the address of a respectable hotel; and I, for my part, put myself under the conduct of Mr. Jones. Before noon of the second Sunday we sighted the low shores outside of New York harbour; the steerage passengers must remain on board to pass through Castle Garden on the following morning; but we of the second cabin made our escape along with the lords of the saloon; and by six o'clock Jones and I issued into West Street, sitting on some straw in the bottom of an open baggage-wagon. It rained miraculously; and from that moment till on the following night I left New York, there was scarce a lull, and no cessation of the downpour. The roadways were flooded; a loud strident noise of falling water filled the air; the restaurants smelt heavily of wet people and wet clothing.

It took us but a few minutes, though it cost us a good deal of money, to be rattled along West Street to our destination: "Reunion House, No. 10 West Street, one minute's walk from Castle Garden; convenient to Castle Garden, the Steamboat Landings, California Steamers and Liverpool Ships; Board and Lodging per day 1 dollar, single meals 25 cents, lodging per night 25 cents; private rooms for families; no charge for storage or baggage; satisfaction guaranteed to all persons; Michael Mitchell,

Proprietor." Reunion House was, I may go the length of saying, a humble hostelry. You entered through a long bar-room, thence passed into a little dining-room, and thence into a still smaller kitchen. The furniture was of the plainest; but the bar was hung in the American taste, with encouraging and hospitable mottoes.

Jones was well known; we were received warmly; and two minutes afterwards I had refused a drink from the proprietor, and was going on, in my plain European fashion, to refuse a cigar, when Mr. Mitchell sternly interposed, and explained the situation. He was offering to treat me, it appeared; whenever an American bar-keeper proposes anything, it must be borne in mind that he is offering to treat; and if I did not want a drink, I must at least take the cigar. I took it bashfully, feeling I had begun my American career on the wrong foot. I did not enjoy that cigar; but this may have been from a variety of reasons, even the best cigar often failing to please if you smoke three-quarters of it in a drenching rain.

For many years America was to me a sort of promised land. " Westward the march of empire holds its way "; the race is for the moment to the young; what has been and what is we imperfectly and obscurely know; what is to be yet lies beyond the flight of our imaginations. Greece, Rome and Judæa are gone by for ever, leaving to generations the legacy of their accomplished work; China still endures, an old-in-

habited house in the brand-new city of nations ;
England has already declined, since she has lost
the States ; and to these States, therefore, yet
undeveloped, full of dark possibilities, and grown,
like another Eve, from one rib out of the side of
their own land, the minds of young men in
England turn naturally at a certain hopeful
period of their age. It will be hard for an
American to understand the spirit. But let
him imagine a young man, who shall have grown
up in an old and rigid circle, following bygone
fashions and taught to distrust his own fresh
instincts, and who now suddenly hears of a
family of cousins, all about his own age, who
keep house together by themselves and live
far from restraint and tradition ; let him imagine
this, and he will have some imperfect notion of
the sentiment with which spirited English youths
turn to the thought of the American Republic.
It seems to them as if, out west, the war of life
was still conducted in the open air, and on free
barbaric terms ; as if it had not yet been narrowed
into parlours, nor begun to be conducted, like
some unjust and dreary arbitration, by com-
promise, costume, forms of procedure, and sad,
senseless self-denial. Which of these two he
prefers, a man with any youth still left in him
will decide rightly for himself. He would rather
be homeless than denied a pass-key ; rather go
without food than partake of a stalled ox in stiff,
respectable society; rather be shot out of hand than
direct his life according to the dictates of the world,

He knows or thinks nothing of the Maine Laws, the Puritan sourness, the fierce, sordid appetite for dollars, or the dreary existence of country towns. A few wild story-books which delighted his childhood form the imaginative basis of his picture of America. In course of time, there is added to this a great crowd of stimulating details—vast cities that grow up as by enchantment; the birds, that have gone south in autumn, returning with the spring to find thousands camped upon their marshes, and the lamps burning far and near along populous streets; forests that disappear like snow; countries larger than Britain that are cleared and settled, one man running forth with his household gods before another, while the bear and the Indian are yet scarce aware of their approach; oil that gushes from the earth; gold that is washed or quarried in the brooks or glens of the Sierras; and all that bustle, courage, action, and constant kaleidoscopic change that Walt Whitman has seized and set forth in his vigorous, cheerful, and loquacious verses.

Here I was at last in America, and was soon out upon New York streets, spying for things foreign. The place had to me an air of Liverpool; but such was the rain that not Paradise itself would have looked inviting. We were a party of four, under two umbrellas; Jones and I and two Scots lads, recent immigrants, and not indisposed to welcome a compatriot. They had been six weeks in New York, and neither of them had yet found a single job or earned a single halfpenny. Up to the present they were exactly out of pocket by the amount of the fare.

The lads soon left us. Now I had sworn by all my gods to have such a dinner as would rouse the dead ; there was scarce any expense at which I should have hesitated ; the devil was in it but Jones and I should dine like heathen emperors. I set to work, asking after a restaurant ; and I chose the wealthiest and most gastronomical-looking passers-by to ask from. Yet, although I had told them I was willing to pay anything in reason, one and all sent me off to cheap, fixed-price houses, where I would not have eaten that night for the cost of twenty dinners. I do not know if this were characteristic of New York, or whether it was only Jones and I who looked un-dienrly and discouraged enterprising suggestions. But at length by our own sagacity, we found a French restaurant, where there was a French waiter, some fair French cooking, some so-called French wine, and French coffee to conclude the whole. I never entered into the feelings of Jack on land so completely as when I tasted that coffee.

I suppose we had one of " private rooms for families " at Reunion House. It was very small, furnished with a bed, a chair, and some clothespegs ; and it derived all that was necessary for the life of the human animal through two borrowed lights : one looking into the passage, and the

second opening, without sash, into another
apartment, where three men fitly snored, or in
intervals of wakefulness, drearily mumbled to
each other all night long. It will be observed
that this was almost exactly the disposition of
the room in M'Naughten's story. Jones had the
bed; I pitched my camp upon the floor; he
did not sleep until near morning, and I, for my
part, never closed an eye.

At sunrise I heard a cannon fired; and shortly
afterwards the men in the next room gave over
snoring for good, and began to rustle over their
toilettes. The sound of their voices as they
talked was low and moaning, like that of people
watching by the sick. Jones, who had at last
begun to doze, tumbled and murmured, and every
now and then opened unconscious eyes upon me
where I lay. I found myself growing eerier and
eerier, for I daresay I was a little fevered by my
restless night, and hurried to dress and get
downstairs.

You had to pass through the rain, which still
fell thick and resonant, to reach a lavatory on
the other side of the court. There were three
basin-stands, and a few crumpled towels and
pieces of wet soap, white and slippery like fish;
nor should I forget a looking-glass and a pair of
questionable combs. Another Scots lad was
here, scrubbing his face with a good will. He had
been three months in New York and had not yet
found a single job nor earned a single halfpenny.
Up to the present, he also was exactly out of

pocket by the amount of the fare. I began to
grow sick at heart for my fellow-emigrants.

Of my nightmare wanderings in New York
I spare to tell. I had a thousand and one
things to do; only the day to do them in, and a
journey across the continent before me in the
evening. It rained with patient fury; every
now and then I had to get under cover for a while
in order, so to speak, to give my mackintosh a
rest; for under this continued drenching it
began to grow damp on the inside. I went to
banks, post-offices, railway-offices, restaurants,
publishers, booksellers, money-changers, and
wherever I went a pool would gather about my
feet, and those who were careful of their
floors would look on with an unfriendly eye.
Wherever I went, too, the same traits struck me :
the people were all surprisingly rude and surprisingly kind. The money-changer cross-ques-
tioned me like a French commissary, asking my
age, my business, my average income, and my
destination, beating down my attempts at
evasion, and receiving my answers in silence ;
and yet when all was over, he shook hands with
me up to the elbows, and sent his lad nearly a
quarter of a mile in the rain to get me books
at a reduction. Again, in a very large publishing
and bookselling establishment a man, who
seemed to be the manager, received me as I had
certainly never before been received in any
human shop, indicated squarely that he put no
faith in my honesty, and refused to look up the

names of books or give me the slightest help of
information, on the ground, like the steward,
that it was none of his business. I lost my
temper at last, said I was a stranger in America
and not learned in their etiquette ; but I would
assure him, if he went to any bookseller in
England, of more handsome usage. The boast
was perhaps exaggerated ; but like many a long
shot, it struck the gold. The manager passed
at once from one extreme to the other ; I may
say that from that moment he loaded me with
kindness ; he gave me all sorts of good advice,
wrote me down addresses, and came bareheaded
into the rain to point me out a restaurant,
where I might lunch, nor even then did he seem
to think that he had done enough. These are
(it is as well to be bold in statement) the manners
of America. It is this same opposition that has
most struck me in people of almost all classes
and from east to west. By the time a man had
about strung me up to be the death of him by
his insulting behaviour, he himself would be
just upon the point of melting into confidence
and   serviceable   attention.   Yet I suspect,
although I have met with the like in so many
parts, that this must be the character of some
particular State or group of States ; for in America
and this again in all classes, you will find some
of the softest-mannered gentlemen in the world.

I was so wet when I got back to Mitchell's
towards the evening, that I had simply to divest
myself of my shoes, socks and trousers, and

leave them behind for the benefit of New York
City. No fire could have dried them ere I had
to start ; and to pack them in their present condition was to spread ruin among my other
possessions. With a heavy heart I said farewell
to them as they lay a pulp in the middle of a
pool upon the floor of Mitchell's kitchen. I
wonder if they are dry by now. Mitchell hired
a man to carry my baggage to the station, which
was hard by, accompanied me thither himself,
and recommended me to the particular attention
of the officials. No one could have been kinder.
Those who are out of pocket may go safely to
Reunion House, where they will get decent meals
and find an honest and obliging landlord. I
owed him this word of thanks, before I enter
fairly on the second and far less agreeable chapter
of my emigrant experience.

ACROSS THE PLAINS

LEAVES FROM THE NOTEBOOK OF AN EMIGRANT BETWEEN NEW YORK AND SAN FRANCISCO

TO

PAUL BOURGET

Traveller and student and curious as you are, you will never have heard the name of Vailima, most likely not even that of Upolu, and Samoa itself may be strange to your ears. To these barbaric seats there came the other day a yellow book with your name on the title, and filled in every page with the exquisite gifts of your art. Let me take and change your own words: J'ai beau admirer les autres de toutes mes forces, c'est avec vous que je me complais à vivre.

R. L. S.

Vailima,
    Upolu,
        Samoa.

LETTER TO THE AUTHOR

(Printed as a preface to *Across the Plains*)

My Dear Stevenson,

You have trusted me with the choice and arrangement of these papers, written before you departed to the South Seas, and have asked me to add a preface to the volume. But it is your prose the public wish to read, not mine ; and I am sure they will willingly be spared the preface. Acknowledgments are due in your name to the publishers of the several magazines from which the papers are collected, viz. *Fraser's, Longman's,* the *Magazine of Art,* and *Scribners'*. I will only add, lest any reader should find the tone of the concluding pieces less inspiriting than your wont, that they were written under circumstances of especial gloom and sickness. " I agree with you the lights seem a little turned down," so you write to me now ; " the truth is I was far through, and came none too soon to the South Seas, where I was to recover peace of body and mind. And however low the lights, the stuff is true. . . ." Well, inasmuch as the South Sea sirens have breathed new life into you, we are bound to be heartily grateful to them, though as they keep you so far removed from us, it is difficult not to bear them a grudge ; and if they would reconcile us quite, they have but to do two things more—to teach you new tales that shall charm us like your old, and to spare you, at least once in a while in summer, to climates within reach of us who are task-bound for ten months in the year beside the Thames.

Yours ever,

SIDNEY COLVIN.

February, 1892.

NOTES BY THE WAY TO COUNCIL BLUFFS

MONDAY.—It was, if I remember rightly, five o'clock when we were all signalled to be present at the Ferry Depot of the railroad. An emigrant ship had arrived at New York on the Saturday night, another on the Sunday morning, our own on Sunday afternoon, a fourth early on Monday ; and as there is no emigrant train on Sunday, a great part of the passengers from these four ships was concentrated on the train by which I was to travel. There was a Babel of bewildered men, women, and children. The wretched little booking-office, and the baggage-room, which was not much larger, were crowded thick with emigrants, and were heavy and rank with the atmosphere of dripping clothes. Open carts full of bedding stood by the half-hour in the rain. The officials loaded each other with recriminations. A bearded, mildewed little man, whom I take to have been an emigrant agent, was all over the place, his mouth full of brimstone, blustering and interfering. It was plain that the whole system, if system there was, had utterly broken down under the strain of so many passengers.

My own ticket was given me at once, and an oldish man, who preserved his head in the midst of this turmoil, got my baggage registered, and counselled me to stay quietly where I was till he should give me the word to move. I had taken along with me a small valise, a knapsack, which I carried on my shoulders, and in the bag of my railway rug the whole of Bancroft's *History of the United States*, in six fat volumes. It was as much as I could carry with convenience even for short distances, but it ensured me plenty of clothing, and the valise was at that moment, and often after, useful for a stool. I am sure I sat an hour in the baggage-room, and wretched enough it was; yet, when at last the word was passed to me and I picked up my bundles and got under way, it was only to exchange discomfort for downright misery and danger.

I followed the porters into a long shed reaching downhill from West Street to the river. It was dark, the wind blew clean through it from end to end; and here I found a great block of passengers and baggage, hundreds of one and tons of the other. I feel I shall have a difficulty to make myself believed; and certainly the scene must have been exceptional, for it was too dangerous for daily repetition. It was a tight jam; there was no fair way through the mingled mass of brute and living obstruction. Into the upper skirts of the crowd, porters, infuriated by hurry and overwork, clove their way with shouts. I may say that we stood like sheep, and that the porters charged among us like so many maddened sheep-dogs; and I

believe these men were no longer answerable for
their acts. It mattered not what they were
carrying, they drove straight into the press, and
when they could get no farther, blindly discharged
their barrowful. With my own hand, for instance, I saved the life of a child as it sat upon
its mother's knee, she sitting on a box; and
since I heard of no accident, I must suppose
that there were many similar interpositions in
the course of the evening. It will give some
idea of the state of mind to which we were
reduced if I tell you that neither the porter nor
the mother of the child paid the least attention
to my act. It was not till some time after that
I understood what I had done myself, for to
ward off heavy boxes seemed at the moment a
natural incident of human life. Cold, wet,
clamour, dead opposition to progress, such as
one encounters in an evil dream, had utterly
daunted the spirits. We had accepted this
purgatory as a child accepts the conditions of
the world. For my part, I shivered a little,
and my back ached wearily; but I believe I
had neither a hope nor a fear, and all the acti-
vities of my nature had become tributary to one
massive sensation of discomfort.

At length, and after how long an interval I
hesitate to guess, the crowd began to move,
heavily straining through itself. About the
same time some lamps were lighted, and threw
a sudden flare over the shed. We were being
filtered out into the river boat for Jersey City.

You may imagine how slowly this filtering proceeded, through the dense, choking crush, every
one overladen with packages or children, and yet
under the necessity of fishing out his ticket by
the way; but it ended at length for me, and I
found myself on deck under a flimsy awning and
with a trifle of elbow-room to stretch and breathe
in. This was on the starboard; for the bulk of
the emigrants stuck hopelessly on the port side,
by which we had entered. In vain the seamen
shouted to them to move on, and threatened
them with shipwreck. These poor people were
under a spell of stupor, and did not stir a foot.
It rained as heavily as ever, but the wind now
came in sudden claps and capfuls, not without
danger to a boat so badly ballasted as ours;
and we crept over the river in the darkness,
trailing one paddle in the water like a wounded
duck, and passed ever and again by huge,
illuminated steamers running many knots, and
heralding their approach by strains of music.
The contrast between these pleasure embarka-
tions and our own grim vessel, with her list to
port and her freight of wet and silent emigrants,
was of that glaring description which we count
too obvious for the purposes of art.

The landing at Jersey was done in a stampede.
I had a fixed sense of calamity, and to judge by
conduct, the same persuasion was common to
us all. A panic selfishness, like that produced
by fear, presided over the disorder of our landing.
People pushed, and elbowed, and ran, their

families following how they could. Children fell, and were picked up to be rewarded by a blow. One child, who had lost her parents, screamed steadily and with increasing shrillness, as though verging towards a fit; an official kept her by him, but no one else seemed so much as to remark her distress; and I am ashamed to say that I ran among the rest. I was so weary that I had twice to make a halt and set down my bundles in the hundred yards or so between the pier and the railway station, so that I was quite wet by the time that I got under cover. There was no waiting-room, no refreshment-room; the cars were locked; and for at least another hour, or so it seemed, we had to camp upon the draughty, gas-lit platform. I sat on my valise, too crushed to observe my neighbours; but as they were all cold, and wet, and weary, and driven stupidly crazy by the mismanagement to which we had been subjected, I believe they can have been no happier than myself. I bought half a dozen oranges from a boy, for oranges and nuts were the only refection to be had. As only two of them had even a pretence of juice, I threw the other four under the cars, and beheld, as in a dream, grown people and children groping on the track after my leavings.

At last we were admitted into the cars, utterly dejected, and far from dry. For my own part, I got out a clothes-brush, and brushed my trousers as hard as I could till I had dried them and warmed my blood into the bargain; but

no one else, except my next neighbour to whom I
lent the brush, appeared to take the least precau-
tion. As they were, they composed themselves
to sleep. I had seen the lights of Philadelphia,
and been twice ordered to change carriages and
twice countermanded, before I allowed myself
to follow their example.

Tuesday.—When I awoke, it was already day ;
the train was standing idle ; I was in the last
carriage, and, seeing some others strolling to
and fro about the lines, I opened the door and
stepped forth, as from a caravan by the wayside.
We were near no station, nor even, as far as I
could see, within reach of any signal. A green,
open, undulating country stretched away upon
all sides. Locust trees and a single field of
Indian corn gave it a foreign grace and interest ;
but the contours of the land were soft and
English. It was not quite England, neither was
it quite France ; yet like enough either to seem
natural in my eyes. And it was in the sky, and
not upon the earth, that I was surprised to find
a change. Explain it how you may, and for my
part I cannot explain it at all, the sun rises with
a different splendour in America and Europe.
There is more clear gold and scarlet in our old
country mornings ; more purple, brown, and
smoky orange in those of the new. It may be
from habit, but to me the coming of day is less
fresh and inspiriting in the latter ; it has a duskier
glory, and more nearly resembles sunset ; it
seems to fit some subsequential, evening epoch of

the world, as though America were in fact, and
not merely in fancy, farther from the orient of
Aurora and the springs of day.   I thought so
then, by the railroad side in Pennsylvania, and
I have thought so a dozen times since in far distant
parts of the continent.   If it be an illusion it is
one very deeply rooted, and in which my eyesight
is accomplice.

Soon after a train whisked by, announcing and
accompanying its passage by the swift beating
of a sort of chapel-bell upon the engine ; and as
it was for this we had been waiting, we were
summoned by the cry of " All aboard ! " and went
on again upon our way.   The whole line, it
appeared, was topsy-turvy ;   an accident at
midnight having thrown all the traffic hours into
arrear.   We paid for this in the flesh, for we had
no meals all that day.   Fruit we could buy
upon the cars ;   and now and then we had a
few minutes at some station with a meagre show
of rolls and sandwiches for sale ; but we were so
many and so ravenous that, though I tried at
every opportunity, the coffee was always exhausted
before I could elbow my way to the counter.

Our American sunrise had ushered in a noble
summer's day.   There was not a cloud ;   the
sunshine was baking ;   yet in the woody river-
valleys among which we wound our way, the
atmosphere preserved a sparkling freshness till
late in the afternoon.   It has an inland sweetness
and variety to one newly from the sea ;   it smelt
of woods, rivers, and the delved earth.   These,

though in so far a country, were airs from home.
I stood on the platform by the hour ; and as I
saw one after another, pleasant villages, carts
upon the highway and fishers by the stream,
and heard cockcrows and cheery voices in the
distance, and beheld the sun, no longer shining
blankly on the plains of ocean, but striking
among shapely hills and his light dispersed and
coloured by a thousand accidents of form and
surface, I began to exult with myself upon this
rise in life like a man who had come into a rich
estate.   And when I had asked the name of a
river from the brakesman, and heard that it
was called the Susquehanna, the beauty of the
name seemed to be part and parcel of the beauty
of the land.   As when Adam with divine fitness
named the creatures, so this word Susquehanna
was at once accepted by the fancy.   That was
the name, as no other could be, for that shining
river and desirable valley.

None can care for literature in itself who do
not take a special pleasure in the sound of names ;
and there is no part of the world where nomen-
clature is so rich, poetical, humorous, and
picturesque as the United States of America.
All times, races, and languages have brought
their contribution.   Pekin is in the same State
with Euclid, with Bellefontaine, and with San-
dusky.   Chelsea, with its London associations of
red brick, Sloane Square, and the King's Road,
is own suburb to stately and primeval Memphis ;
there they have their seat, translated names of

cities, where the Mississippi runs by Tennessee and Arkansas ; * and both, while I was crossing the continent, lay, watched by armed men, in the horror and isolation of a plague. Old, red Manhattan lies, like an Indian arrow-head under a steam factory, below Anglified New York. The names of the States and Territories themselves form a chorus of sweet and most romantic vocables : Delaware, Ohio, Indiana, Florida, Dakota, Iowa, Wyoming, Minnesota, and the Carolinas ; there are few poems with a nobler music for the ear : a songful, tuneful land ; and if the new Homer shall arise from the Western continent, his verse will be enriched, his pages sing spontaneously, with the names of states and cities that would strike the fancy in a business circular.

Late in the evening we were landed in a waiting-room at Pittsburg. I had now under my charge a young and sprightly Dutch widow with her children ; these I was to watch over providentially for a certain distance farther on the way ; but as I found she was furnished with a basket of eatables, I left her in the waiting-room to seek a dinner for myself.

I mention this meal, not only because it was the first of which I had partaken for about thirty hours, but because it was the means of my first introduction to a coloured gentleman. He did me the honour to wait upon me after a fashion, while I was eating ; and with every word, look,

* Please pronounce Arkansaw, with the accent on the first.

and gesture marched me farther into the country of surprise. He was indeed strikingly unlike the negroes of Mrs. Beecher Stowe, or the Christy Minstrels of my youth. Imagine a gentleman, certainly somewhat dark, but of a pleasant warm hue, speaking English with a slight and rather odd foreign accent, every inch a man of the world, and armed with manners so patronisingly superior that I am at a loss to name their parallel in England. A butler perhaps rides as high over the unbutlered, but then he sets you right with a reserve and a sort of sighing patience which one is often moved to admire. And again, the abstract butler never stoops to familiarity. But the coloured gentleman will pass you a wink at a time ; he is familiar like an upper-form boy to a fag ; he unbends to you like Prince Hal with Poins and Falstaff. He makes himself at home and welcome. Indeed, I may say, this waiter behaved himself to me throughout that supper much as, with us, a young, free, and not very self-respecting master might behave to a good-looking chambermaid. I had come prepared to pity the poor negro, to put him at his ease, to prove in a thousand condescensions that I was no sharer in the prejudice of race ; but I assure you I put my patronage away for another occasion, and had the grace to be pleased with that result.

Seeing he was a very honest fellow, I consulted him upon a point of etiquette : if one should offer to tip the American waiter ? Certainly not, he told me. Never. It would not do. They considered themselves too highly to accept. They would even resent the offer. As for him and me, we had enjoyed a very pleasant conversation; he, in particular, had found much pleasure in my society; I was a stranger; this was exactly one of those rare conjunctures. . . . Without being very clear-seeing, I can still perceive the sun at noonday; and the coloured gentleman deftly pocketed a quarter.

Wednesday.—A little after midnight I convoyed my widow and orphans on board the train; and morning found us far into Ohio. This had early been a favourite home of my imagination; I have played at being in Ohio by the week, and enjoyed some capital sport there with a dummy gun, my person being still unbreeched. My preference was founded on a work which appeared in *Cassell's Family Paper*, and was read aloud to me by my nurse. It narrated the doings of one Custaloga, an Indian brave, who, in the last chapter, very obligingly washed the paint off his face and became Sir Reginald Somebody-or-other; a trick I never forgave him. The idea of a man being an Indian brave, and then giving up that to be a baronet, was one which my mind rejected. It offended verisimilitude, like the pretended anxiety of Robinson Crusoe and others to escape from uninhabited islands.

But Ohio was not at all as I had pictured it. We were now on those great plains which stretch unbroken to the Rocky Mountains. The country

was flat like Holland, but far from being dull.
All through Ohio, Indiana, Illinois, and Iowa, or
for as much as I saw of them from the train and
in my waking moments, it was rich and various,
and breathed an elegance peculiar to itself.
The tall corn pleased the eye; the trees were
graceful in themselves, and framed the plain into
long, aerial vistas; and the clean, bright,
gardened townships spoke of country fare and
pleasant summer evenings on the stoop. It was
a sort of flat paradise; but, I am afraid, not
unfrequented by the devil. That morning
dawned with such a freezing chill as I have rarely
felt; a chill that was not perhaps so measurable
by instrument, as it struck home upon the
heart and seemed to travel with the blood. Day
came in with a shudder. White mists lay thinly
over the surface of the plain, as we see them
more often on a lake; and though the sun had
soon dispersed and drunk them up, leaving an
atmosphere of fever-heat and crystal pureness
from horizon to horizon, the mists had still been
there, and we knew that this paradise was
haunted by killing damps and foul malaria.
The fences along the line bore but two descrip-
tions of advertisement; one to recommend
tobaccos, and the other to vaunt remedies
against the ague. At the point of day, and while
we were all in the grasp of that first chill, a native
of the State, who had got in at some way-station,
pronounced it, with a doctoral air, " a fever and
ague morning."

The Dutch widow was a person of some character. She had conceived at first sight a great aversion for the present writer, which she was at no pains to conceal. But, being a woman of a practical spirit, she made no difficulty about accepting my attentions, and encouraged me to buy her children fruits and candies, to carry all her parcels, and even to sleep upon the floor that she might profit by my empty seat. Nay, she was such a rattle by nature, and so powerfully moved to autobiographical talk, that she was forced, for want of a better, to take me into confidence and tell me the story of her life. I heard about her late husband, who seemed to have made his chief impression by taking her out pleasuring on Sundays. I could tell you her prospects, her hopes, the amount of her fortune, the cost of her housekeeping by the week, and a variety of particular matters that are not usually disclosed except to friends. At one station she shook up her children to look at a man on the platform and say if he were not like Mr. Z.; while to me she explained how she had been keeping company with this Mr. Z., how far matters had proceeded, and how it was because of his desistance that she was now travelling to the west. Then, when I was thus put in possession of the facts, she asked my judgment on that type of manly beauty. I admired it to her heart's content. She was not, I think, remarkably veracious in talk but broidered as fancy prompted, and built castles in the air out of her past ; yet she had that sort of candour, to keep me, in spite of all these confidences, steadily aware of her aversion. Her parting words were ingeniously honest. " I am sure," said she, " we all *ought* to be very much obliged to you." I cannot pretend that she put me at my ease ; but I had a certain respect for such a genuine dislike. A poor nature would have slipped, in the course of these familiarities, into a sort of worthless toleration for me.

We reached Chicago in the evening. I was turned out of the cars, bundled into an omnibus, and driven off through the streets to the station of a different railroad. Chicago seemed a great and gloomy city. I remember having subscribed, let us say sixpence, towards its restoration at the period of the fire ; and now when I beheld street after street of ponderous houses and crowds of comfortable burghers, I thought it would be a graceful act for the corporation to refund that sixpence, or, at the least, to entertain me to a cheerful dinner. But there was no word of restitution. I was that city's benefactor, yet I was received in a third-class waiting-room, and the best dinner I could get was a dish of ham and eggs at my own expense.

I can safely say, I have never been so dog-tired as that night in Chicago. When it was time to start, I descended the platform like a man in a dream. It was a long train, lighted from end to end ; and car after car, as I came up with it, was not only filled but overflowing. My valise, my knapsack, my rug, with those six ponderous tomes of Bancroft, weighed me double ; I was hot, feverish, painfully athirst ; and there was a great darkness over me, an internal darkness, not to be dispelled by gas. When at last I found an empty bench, I sank into it like a bundle of rags, the world seemed to swim away into the distance, and my consciousness dwindled within me to a mere pin's head, like a taper on a foggy night.

When I came a little more to myself, I found that there had sat down beside me a very cheerful rosy little German gentleman, somewhat gone in drink, who was talking away to me, nineteen to the dozen, as they say. I did my best to keep up the conversation ; for it seemed to me dimly as if something depended upon that. I heard him relate, among many other things, that there were pickpockets on the train, who had already robbed a man of forty dollars and a return ticket ; but though I caught the words, I do not think I properly understood the sense until next morning ; and I believe I replied at the time that I was very glad to hear it. What else he talked about I have no guess ; I remember a gabbling sound of words, his profuse gesticulation, and his smile, which was highly explanatory ; but no more. And I suppose I must have shown my confusion very plainly ; for, first, I saw him knit his brows at me like one who has conceived a doubt ; next, he tried me in German, supposing perhaps that I was unfamiliar with the English

tongue ; and finally, in despair, he rose and left
me.   I felt chagrined ; but my fatigue was too
crushing for delay, and, stretching myself as far
as that was possible upon the bench, I was
received at once into a dreamless stupor.

The little German gentleman was only going
a little way into the suburbs after a *dîner fin*,
and was bent on entertainment while the journey
lasted.   Having failed with me, he pitched next
upon another emigrant, who had come through
from Canada, and was not one jot less weary
than myself.   Nay, even in a natural state, as I
found next morning when we scraped acquaintance, he was a heavy, uncommunicative man.
After trying him on different topics, it appears
that the little German gentleman flounced into
a temper, swore an oath or two, and departed
from that car in quest of livelier society.   Poor
little gentleman ! I suppose he thought an
emigrant should be a rollicking, free-hearted
blade, with a flask of foreign brandy and a long,
comical story to beguile the moments of digestion.

Thursday.—I suppose there must be a cycle in
the fatigue of travelling, for when I awoke next
morning, I was entirely renewed in spirits and
ate a hearty breakfast of porridge, with sweet
milk, and coffee and hot cakes at Burlington,
upon the Mississippi.   Another long day's ride
followed, with but one feature worthy of remark.
At a place called Creston, a drunken man got in.
He was aggressively friendly, but, according to
English notions, not at all unpresentable upon a

train. For one stage he eluded the notice of
the officials ; but just as we were beginning to
move out of the next station, Cromwell by name,
by came the conductor. There was a word or
two of talk ; and then the official had the man
by the shoulders, twitched him from his seat,
marched him through the car, and sent him
flying on to the track. It was done in three
motions, as exact as a piece of drill. The train
was still moving slowly, although beginning to
mend her pace, and the drunkard got his feet
without a fall. He carried a red bundle, though
not so red as his cheeks ; and he shook this menac-
ingly in the air with one hand, while the other
stole behind him to the region of the kidneys.
It was the first indication that I had come among
revolvers, and I observed it with some emotion.
The conductor stood on the steps with one hand
on his hip, looking back at him ; and perhaps
this attitude imposed upon the creature, for he
turned without further ado, and went off stag-
gering along the track towards Cromwell, followed by a peal of laughter from the cars.
They were speaking English all about me, but I
knew I was in a foreign land.

Twenty minutes before nine that night we were
deposited at the Pacific Transfer Station near
Council Bluffs, on the eastern banks of the
Missouri river. Here we were to stay the night
at a kind of caravanserai, set apart for emigrants.
But I gave way to a thirst for luxury, separated
myself from my companions, and marched with

xx   K

my effects into the Union Pacific Hotel. A white clerk and a coloured gentleman whom, in my plain European way, I should call the boots, were installed behind a counter like bank tellers. They took my name, assigned me a number, and proceeded to deal with my packages. And here came the tug of war. I wished to give up my packages into safe keeping ; but I did not wish to go to bed. And this, it appeared, was impossible in an American hotel.

It was, of course, some inane misunderstanding, and sprang from my unfamiliarity with the language. For although two nations use the same words and read the same books, intercourse is not conducted by the dictionary. The business of life is not carried on by words, but in set phrases, each with a special and almost a slang signification. Some international obscurity prevailed between me and the coloured gentleman at Council Bluffs ; so that what I was asking, which seemed very natural to me, appeared to him a monstrous exigency. He refused, and that with the plainness of the West. This American manner of conducting matters of business is, at first, highly unpalatable to the European. When we approach a man in the way of his calling, and for those services by which he earns his bread, we consider him for the time being our hired servant. But in the American opinion, two gentlemen meet and have a friendly talk with a view to exchanging favours if they shall agree to please. I know not which is the more convenient, nor even which is the more truly courteous. The English stiffness unfortunately tends to be continued after the particular transaction is at an end, and thus favours class separations. But on the other hand these equalitarian plainnesses leave an open field for the insolence of Jack-in-office.

I was nettled by the coloured gentleman's refusal, and unbottoned my wrath under the similitude of ironical submission. I knew nothing, I said, of the ways of American hotels; but I had no desire to give trouble. If there was nothing for it but to get to bed immediately, let him say the word, and though it was not my habit, I should cheerfully obey.

He burst into a shout of laughter. " Ah ! " said he, " you do not know about America. They are fine people in America. Oh ! you will like them very well. But you mustn't get mad. I know what you want. You come along with me."

And issuing from behind the counter, and taking me by the arm like an old acquaintance, he led me to the bar of the hotel.

" There," said he, pushing me from him by the shoulder, " go and have a drink ! "

THE EMIGRANT TRAIN

ALL this while I had been travelling by mixed trains, where I might meet with Dutch widows and little German gentry fresh from table. I had been but a latent emigrant ; now I was to be branded once more, and put apart from my fellows. It was about two in the afternoon of Friday that I found myself in front of the Emigrant House, with more than a hundred others, to be sorted and boxed for the journey. A white-haired official, with a stick under one arm, and a list in the other hand, stood apart in front of us, and called name after name in the tone of a command. At each name you would see a family gather up its brats and bundles and run for the hindmost of the three cars that stood awaiting us, and I soon concluded that this was to be set apart for the women and children. The second or central car, it turned out, was devoted to men travelling alone, and the third to the Chinese. The official was easily moved to anger at the least delay ; but the emigrants were both quick at answering their names, and speedy in getting themselves and their effects on board.

The families once housed, we men carried the second car without ceremony by simultaneous

assault. I suppose the reader has some notion
of an American railroad-car, that long, narrow
wooden box, like a flat-roofed Noah's ark, with
a stove and a convenience, one at either end,
a passage down the middle, and transverse
benches upon either hand. Those destined for
emigrants on the Union Pacific are only remarkable for their extreme plainness, nothing but
wood entering in any part into their constitution,
and for the usual inefficacy of the lamps, which
often went out and shed but a dying glimmer
even while they burned. The benches are too
short for anything but a young child. Where
there is scarce elbow-room for two to sit, there
will not be space enough for one to lie. Hence
the company, or rather, as it appears from certain
bills about the Transfer Station, the company's
servants, have conceived a plan for the better
accommodation of travellers. They prevail on
every two to chum together. To each of the
chums they sell a board and three square cushions
stuffed with straw, and covered with thin cotton.
The benches can be made to face each other in
pairs, for the backs are reversible. On the
approach of night the boards are laid from
bench to bench, making a couch wide enough for
two, and long enough for a man of the middle
height; and the chums lie down side by side
upon the cushions with the head to the conductor's
van and the feet to the engine. When the train
is full, of course this plan is impossible, for there
must not be more than one to every bench,

neither can it be carried out unless the chums agree. It was to bring about this last condition that our white-haired official now bestirred himself. He made a most active master of ceremonies, introducing likely couples, and even guaranteeing the amiability and honesty of each. The greater number of happy couples the better for his pocket, for it was he who sold the raw material of the beds. His price for one board and three straw cushions began with two dollars and a half; but before the train left, and, I am sorry to say long after I had purchased mine, it had fallen to one dollar and a half.

The match-maker had a difficulty with me; perhaps, like some ladies, I showed myself too eager for union at any price; but certainly the first who was picked out to be my bedfellow, declined the honour without thanks. He was an old, heavy, slow-spoken man, I think from Yankeeland, looked me all over with great timidity, and then began to excuse himself in broken phrases. He didn't know the young man, he said. The young man might be very honest, but how was he to know that? There was another young man whom he had met already in the train; he guessed *he* was honest, and would prefer to chum with *him* upon the whole. All this without any sort of excuse, as though I had been inanimate or absent. I began to tremble lest every one should refuse my company, and I be left rejected. But the next in turn was a tall, strapping, long-limbed, small-headed, curly-haired Pennsylvania Dutchman, with a soldierly smartness in his manner. To be exact, he had acquired it in the navy. But that was all one; he had at least been trained to desperate resolves, so he accepted the match, and the white-haired swindler pronounced the connubial benediction, and pocketed his fees.

The rest of the afternoon was spent in making up the train. I am afraid to say how many baggage-waggons followed the engine—certainly a score; then came the Chinese, then we, then the families, and the rear was brought up by the conductor in what, if I have it rightly, is called his caboose. The class to which I belonged was of course far the largest, and we ran over, so to speak, to both sides; so that there were some Caucasians among the Chinamen, and some bachelors among the families. But our own car was pure from admixture, save for one little boy of eight or nine, who had the whooping-cough. At last, about six, the long train crawled out of the Transfer Station and across the wide Missouri river to Omaha, westward bound.

It was a troubled uncomfortable evening in the cars. There was thunder in the air, which helped to keep us restless. A man played many airs upon the cornet, and none of them were much attended to, until he came to " Home, sweet Home." It was truly strange to note how the talk ceased at that, and the faces began to lengthen. I have no idea whether musically

this air is to be considered good or bad ; but it
belongs to that class of art which may be best
described as a brutal assault upon the feelings.
Pathos must be relieved by dignity of treatment.
If you wallow naked in the pathetic, like the
author of " Home, sweet Home," you make your
hearers weep in an unmanly fashion ; and even
while yet they are moved, they despise themselves and hate the occasion of their weakness.
It did not come to tears that night, for the
experiment was interrupted. An elderly, hard-
looking man, with a goatee beard and about as
much appearance of sentiment as you would
expect from a retired slaver, turned with a start
and bade the performer stop that " damned
thing." " I've heard about enough of that,"
he added ; " give us something about the good
country we're going to." A murmur of adhesion
ran round the car ; the performer took the
instrument from his lips, laughed and nodded,
and then struck into a dancing measure ; and,
like a new Timotheus, stilled immediately the
emotion he had raised.

The day faded ; the lamps were lit ; a party of
wild young men, who got off next evening at
North Platte, stood together on the stern platform, singing " The Sweet By-and-bye " with
very tuneful voices ; the chums began to put up
their beds ; and it seemed as if the business of
the day were at an end. But it was not so ; for,
the train stopping at some station, the cars were
instantly thronged with the natives, wives and

fathers, young men and maidens, some of them in little more than nightgear, some with stable lanterns, and all offering beds for sale. Their charge began with twenty-five cents a cushion, but fell, before the train went on again, to fifteen, with the bed-board gratis, or less than one-fifth of what I had paid for mine at the Transfer. This is my contribution to the economy of future emigrants.

A great personage on an American train is the newsboy. He sells books (such books !), papers, fruit, lollipops, and cigars ; and on emigrant journeys, soap, towels, tin washing-dishes, tin coffee pitchers, coffee, tea, sugar, and tinned eatables, mostly hash or beans and bacon. Early next morning the newsboy went around the cars, and chumming on a more extended principle became the order of the hour. It requires but a co-partnery of two to manage beds ; but washing and eating can be carried on most economically by a syndicate of three. I myself entered a little after sunrise into articles of agreement, and became one of the firm of Pennsylvania, Shakespeare, and Dubuque. Shakespeare was my own nickname on the cars ; Pennsylvania that of my bedfellow ; and Dubuque, the name of a place in the State of Iowa, that of an amiable young fellow going west to cure an asthma, and retarding his recovery by incessantly chewing or smoking, and sometimes chewing and smoking together. I have never seen tobacco so sillily abused. Shakespeare bought a tin washing-dish, Dubuque a towel, and Pennsylvania a brick of soap. The partners used these instruments, one after another, according to the order of their first awaking ; and when the firm had finished there was no want of borrowers. Each filled the tin dish at the water filter opposite the stove, and retired with the whole stock in trade to the platform of the car. There he knelt down, supporting himself by a shoulder against the woodwork ; or one elbow crooked about the railing, and made a shift to wash his face and neck and hands—a cold, an insufficient, and, if the train is moving rapidly, a somewhat dangerous toilet.

On a similar division of expense, the firm of Pennsylvania, Shakespeare, and Dubuque supplied themselves with coffee, sugar, and necessary vessels ; and their operations are a type of what went on through all the cars. Before the sun was up the stove would be brightly burning ; at the first station the natives would come on board with milk and eggs and coffee-cakes; and soon from end to end the car would be filled with little parties breakfasting upon the bed-boards. It was the pleasantest hour of the day.

There were meals to be had, however, by the wayside : a breakfast in the morning, a dinner somewhere between eleven and two, and supper from five to eight or nine at night. We had rarely less than twenty minutes for each ; and if we had not spent many another twenty minutes waiting for some express upon a side track among miles of desert, we might have taken an hour to each repast and arrived at San Francisco up to time. For haste is not the foible of an emigrant train. It gets through on sufferance, running the gauntlet among its more considerable brethren; should there be a block, it is unhesitatingly sacrificed; and they cannot, in consequence, predict the length of the passage within a day or so. Civility is the main comfort that you miss. Equality, though conceived very largely in America, does not extend so low down as to an emigrant. Thus in all other trains, a warning cry of " All aboard ! " recalls the passengers to take their seats ; but as soon as I was alone with emigrants, and from the Transfer all the way to San Francisco, I found this ceremony was pretermitted ; the train stole from the station without note of warning, and you had to keep an eye upon it even while you ate. The annoyance is considerable, and the disrespect both wanton and petty.

Many conductors, again, will hold no communication with an emigrant. I asked a conductor one day at what time the train would stop for dinner ; as he made no answer I repeated the question, with a like result ; a third time I returned to the charge, and then Jack-in-office looked me coolly in the face for several seconds and turned ostentatiously away. I believe he was half-ashamed of his brutality ; for when another person made the same inquiry, although he still refused the information, he condescended to answer, and even to justify his reticence in a voice loud enough for me to hear. It was, he said, his principle not to tell people where they were to dine ; for one answer led to many other questions, as what o'clock it was ? or, how soon should we be there ? and he could not afford to be eternally worried.

As you are thus cut off from the superior authorities, a great deal of your comfort depends on the character of the newsboy. He has it in his power indefinitely to better and brighten the emigrant's lot. The newsboy with whom we started from the Transfer was a dark, bullying, contemptuous, insolent scoundrel, who treated us like dogs. Indeed, in his case, matters came nearly to a fight. It happened thus : he was going his rounds through the cars with some commodities for sale, and coming to a party who were at Seven-up or Cascino (our two games), upon a bed-board, slung down a cigar-box in the middle of the cards, knocking one man's hand to the floor. It was the last straw. In a moment the whole party were upon their feet, the cigars were upset, and he was ordered to " get out of that directly, or he would get more than he reckoned for." The fellow grumbled and muttered, but ended by making off, and was less openly insulting in the future. On the other hand, the lad who rode with us in this capacity from Ogden to Sacramento made himself the friend of all, and helped us with informa-

tion, attention, assistance, and a kind countenance. He told us where and when we should
have our meals, and how long the train would
stop; kept seats at table for those who were
delayed, and watched that we should neither be
left behind nor yet unnecessarily hurried. You,
who live at home at ease, can hardly realise the
greatness of this service, even had it stood alone.
When I think of that lad coming and going,
train after train, with his bright face and civil
words, I see how easily a good man may become
the benefactor of his kind. Perhaps he is discontented with himself, perhaps troubled with
ambitions; why, if he but knew it, he is a hero
of the old Greek stamp; and while he thinks he
is only earning a profit of a few cents, and that
perhaps exorbitant, he is doing a man's work, and
bettering the world.

I must tell here an experience of mine with
another newsboy. I tell it because it gives so
good an example of that uncivil kindness of the
American, which is perhaps their most bewilder-
ing character to one newly landed. It was
immediately after I had left the emigrant train;
and I am told I looked like a man at death's door,
so much had this long journey shaken me. I sat
at the end of a car, and the catch being broken,
and myself feverish and sick, I had to hold the
door open with my foot for the sake of air. In
this attitude my leg debarred the newsboy from
his box of merchandise. I made haste to let
him pass when I observed that he was coming;

but I was busy with a book, and so once or twice he came upon me unawares. On these occasions he most rudely struck my foot aside ; and though I myself apologised, as if to show him the way, he answered me never a word. I chafed furiously, and I fear the next time it would have come to words. But suddenly I felt a touch upon my shoulder, and a large juicy pear was put into my hand. It was the newsboy, who had observed that I was looking ill and so made me this present out of a tender heart. For the rest of the journey I was petted like a sick child ; he lent me newspapers, thus depriving himself of his legitimate profit on their sale, and came repeatedly to sit by me and cheer me up.

THE PLAINS OF NEBRASKA

IT had thundered on the Friday night, but the sun rose on Saturday without a cloud. We were at sea—there is no other adequate expression—on the plains of Nebraska. I made my observatory on the top of a fruit-waggon, and sat by the hour upon that perch to spy about me, and to spy in vain for something new. It was a world almost without a feature ; an empty sky, an empty earth ; front and back, the line of railway stretched from horizon to horizon, like a cue across a billiard-board ; on either hand, the green plain ran till it touched the skirts of heaven. Along the track innumerable wild sunflowers, no bigger than a crown-piece, bloomed in a continuous flower-bed ; grazing beasts were seen upon the prairie at all degree of distance and diminution ; and, now and again we might perceive a few dots beside the railroad which grew more and more distinct as we drew nearer till they turned into wooden cabins, and then dwindled and dwindled in our wake until they melted into their surroundings, and we were once more alone upon the billiard-board. The train toiled over this infinity like a snail ; and being the one thing moving, it was wonderful what huge proportions it began to assume in our regard. It

seemed miles in length, and either end of it
within but a step of the horizon. Even my own
body or my own head seemed a great thing in
that emptiness. I note the feeling the more
readily as it is the contrary of what I have read
of in the experience of others. Day and night,
above the roar of the train, our ears were kept
busy with the incessant chirp of grasshoppers—
a noise like the winding up of countless clocks
and watches, which began after a while to seem
proper to that land.

To one hurrying through by steam there was
a certain exhilaration in this spacious vacancy,
this greatness of the air, this discovery of the
whole arch of heaven, this straight, unbroken
prison-line of the horizon. Yet one could not but
reflect upon the weariness of those who passed
by there in old days, at the foot's pace of oxen,
painfully urging their teams, and with no land-
mark but that unattainable evening sun for
which they steered, and which daily fled them by
an equal stride. They had nothing, it would
seem, to overtake; nothing by which to reckon
their advance; no sight for repose or for encouragement; but stage after stage, only the dead
green waste under foot, and the mocking, fugitive
horizon. But the eye, as I have been told, found
differences even here; and at the worst the
emigrant came, by perseverance, to the end of
his toil. It is the settlers, after all, at whom
we have a right to marvel. Our consciousness,
by which we live, is itself but the creature of

variety. Upon what food does it subsist in
such a land ? What livelihood can repay a
human creature for a life spent in this huge
sameness ? He is cut off from books, from news,
from company, from all that can relieve existence
but the prosecution of his affairs. A sky full of
stars is the most varied spectacle that he can
hope. He may walk five miles and see nothing ;
ten, and it is as though he had not moved ;
twenty, and still he is in the midst of the same
great level, and has approached no nearer to the
one object within view, the flat horizon which
keeps pace with his advance. We are full at
home of the question of agreeable wall-papers,
and wise people are of opinion that the temper
may be quieted by sedative surroundings. But
what is to be said of the Nebraskan settler ?
His is a wall-paper with a vengeance—one quarter
of the universe laid bare in all its gauntness.
His eyes must embrace at every glance the
whole seeming concave of the visible world ;
it quails before so vast an outlook, it is tortured
by distance ; yet there is no rest or shelter, till
the man runs into his cabin, and can repose his
sight upon things near at hand. Hence, I am
told, a sickness of the vision peculiar to these
empty plains.

Yet perhaps with sunflowers and cicadæ,
summer and winter, cattle, wife and family, the
settler may create a full and various existence.
One person at least I saw upon the plains who
seemed in every way superior to her lot. This

was a woman who boarded us at a way-station,
selling milk. She was largely formed; her
features were more than comely; she had that
great rarity—a fine complexion which became
her; and her eyes were kind, dark, and steady.
She sold milk with patriarchal grace. There was
not a line in her countenance, not a note in her
soft and sleepy voice, but spoke of an entire con-
tentment with her life. It would have been
fatuous arrogance to pity such a woman. Yet
the place where she lived was to me almost
ghastly. Less than a dozen wooden houses,
all of a shape and all nearly of a size, stood
planted along the railway lines. Each stood
apart in its own lot. Each opened direct off
the billiard-board, as if it were a billiard-board
indeed, and these only models that had been set
down upon it ready-made. Her own, into which
I looked, was clean but very empty, and showed
nothing home-like but the burning fire. This
extreme newness, above all in so naked and flat
a country, gives a strong impression of arti-
ficiality. With none of the litter and discolora-
tion of human life; with the paths unworn, and
the houses still sweating from the axe, such a
settlement as this seems purely scenic. The mind
is loth to accept it for a piece of reality; and it
seems incredible that life can go on with so few
properties, or the great child, man, find entertainment in so bare a play-room.

And truly it is as yet an incomplete society in
some points; or at least it contained, as I passed

through, one person incompletely civilised. At North Platte, where we supped that evening, one man asked another to pass the milk-jug. This other was well-dressed and of what we should call a respectable appearance; a darkish man, high spoken, eating as though he had some usage of society; but he turned upon the first speaker with extraordinary vehemence of tone——

" There's a waiter here ! " he cried.

" I only asked you to pass the milk," explained the first.

Here is the retort verbatim——

" Pass ! Hell ! I'm not paid for that business ; the waiter's paid for it. You should use civility at table, and, by God, I'll show you how ! "

The other man very wisely made no answer, and the bully went on with his supper as though nothing had occurred. It pleases me to think that some day soon he will meet with one of his own kidney ; and that perhaps both may fall.

THE DESERT OF WYOMING

TO cross such a plain is to grow home-sick for the mountains. I longed for the Black Hills of Wyoming, which I knew we were soon to enter, like an ice-bound whaler for the spring. Alas ! and it was a worse country than the other. All Sunday and Monday we travelled through these sad mountains, or over the main ridge of the Rockies, which is a fair match to them for misery of aspect. Hour after hour it was the same unhomely and unkindly world about our onward path ; tumbled boulders, cliffs that drearily imitate the shape of monuments and fortifications—how drearily, how tamely, none can tell who has not seen them ; not a tree, not a patch of sward, not one shapely or commanding mountain form ; sage-brush, eternal sage-brush ; over all, the same weariful and gloomy colouring, greys warming into brown, greys darkening towards black ; and for sole sign of life, here and there a few fleeing antelopes ; here and there, but at incredible intervals, a creek running in a cañon. The plains have a grandeur of their own ; but here there is nothing but a contorted smallness. Except for the air, which was light and stimulating, there was not one good circumstance in that God-forsaken land.

I had been suffering in my health a good deal all the way ; and at last, whether I was exhausted by my complaint or poisoned in some wayside eating-house, the evening we left Laramie, I fell sick outright. That was a night which I shall not readily forget. The lamps did not go out ; each made a faint shining in its own neighbourhood, and the shadows were confounded together in the long, hollow box of the car. The sleepers lay in uneasy attitudes ; here two chums alongside, flat upon their backs like dead folk ; there a man sprawling on the floor, with his face upon his arm ; there another half-seated with his head and shoulders on the bench. The most passive were continually and roughly shaken by the movement of the train ; others stirred, turned, or stretched out their arms like children ; it was surprising how many groaned and murmured in their sleep ; and as I passed to and fro, stepping across the prostrate, and caught now a snore, now a gasp, now a half-formed word, it gave me a measure of the worthlessness of rest in that unresting vehicle. Although it was chill, I was obliged to open my window, for the degradation of the air soon became intolerable to one who was awake and using the full supply of life. Outside, in a glimmering night, I saw the black, amorphous hills shoot by unweariedly into our wake. They that long for morning have never longed for it more earnestly than I.

And yet when day came, it was to shine upon the same broken and unsightly quarter of the

world. Mile upon mile, and not a tree, a bird,
or a river. Only down the long, sterile cañons,
the train shot hooting and awoke the resting
echo. That train was the one piece of life in
all the deadly land ; it was the one actor, the one
spectacle fit to be observed in this paralysis of
man and nature. And when I think how the
railroad has been pushed through this un-
watered wilderness and haunt of savage tribes,
and now will bear an emigrant for some twelve
pounds from the Atlantic to the Golden Gates ;
how at each stage of the construction, roaring,
impromptu cities, full of gold and lust and death,
sprang up and then died away again, and are
now but wayside stations in the desert ; how in
these uncouth places pig-tailed Chinese pirates
worked side by side with border ruffians and
broken men from Europe, talking together in a
mixed dialect, mostly oaths, gambling, drinking,
quarrelling and murdering like wolves ; how the
plumed hereditary lord of all America heard, in
this last fastness, the scream of the " bad
medicine-waggon " charioting his foes ; and
then when I go on to remember that all this
epical turmoil was conducted by gentlemen in
frock coats, and with a view to nothing more
extraordinary than a fortune and a subsequent
visit to Paris, it seems to me, I own, as if this
railway were the one typical achievement of the
age in which we live, as if it brought together
into one plot all the ends of the world and all
the degrees of social rank, and offered to some

great writer the busiest, the most extended, and the most varied subject for an enduring literary work. If it be romance, if it be contrast, if it be heroism that we require, what was Troy town to this ? But, alas ! it is not these things that are necessary—it is only Homer.

Here also we are grateful to the train, as to some god who conducts us swiftly through these shades and by so many hidden perils. Thirst, hunger, the sleight and ferocity of Indians are all no more feared, so lightly do we skim these horrible lands ; as the gull, who wings safely through the hurricane and past the shark. Yet we should not be forgetful of these hardships of the past ; and to keep the balance true, since I have complained of the trifling discomforts of my journey, perhaps more than was enough, let me add an original document. It was not written by Homer, but by a boy of eleven, long since dead, and is dated only twenty years ago. I shall punctuate, to make things clearer, but not change the spelling.

" *My dear sister Mary,—I am afraid you will go nearly crazy when you read my letter. If Jerry* " (*the writer's eldest brother*) " *has not written to you before now, you will be surprised to heare that we are in California, and that poor Thomas* " (*another brother, of fifteen*) " *is dead. We started from —— in July, with plenty of provisions and too yoke oxen. We went along very well till we got within six or seven hundred miles of California, when the Indians attacked us. We found places where they had killed the emigrants. We had one passenger with us, too guns, and one revolver; so we ran all the lead We had into bullets (and) hung the guns up in the wagon so that we could get at them in a minit. It was about two o'clock in the afternoon; droave the cattel a little way; when a prairie chicken alited a little way from the wagon.*

" Jerry took out one of the guns to shoot it, and told Tom to drive the oxen. Tom and I drove the oxen, and Jerry and the passenger went on. Then, after a little, I left Tom and caught up with Jerry and the other man. Jerry stopped for Tom to come up; me and the man went on and sit down by a little stream. In a few minutes, we heard some noise; then three shots (they all struck poor Tom, I suppose); then they gave the war hoop, and as many as twenty of the red skins came down upon us. The three that shot Tom was hid by the side of the road in the bushes.

" I thought the Tom and Jerry were shot; so I told the other man that Tom and Jerry were dead, and that we had better try to escape, if possible. I had no shoes on; having a sore foot, I thought I would not put them on. The man and me run down the road, but We was soon stopt by an Indian on a pony. We then turned the other way, and run up the side of the Mountain, and hid behind some cedar trees, and stayed there till dark. The Indians hunted all over after us, and verry close to us, so close that we could here there tomyhawks Jingle. At dark the man and me started on, I stubing my

toes against sticks and stones. We traveld on all night; and next morning, Just as it was getting gray, we saw something in the shape of a man. It layed Down in the grass. We went up to it, and it was Jerry. He thought we ware Indians. You can imagine how glad he was to see me. He thought we was all dead but him, and we thought him and Tom was dead. He had the gun that he took out of the wagon to shoot the prairie Chicken; all he had was the load that was in it.

" We traveld on till about eight o'clock, We caught up with one wagon with too men in it. We had traveld with them before one day; we stopt and they Drove on; we knew that they was ahead of us, unless they had been killed to. My feet was so sore when we caught up with them that I had to ride; I could not step. We traveld on for two days, when the men that owned the cattle said they would (could) not drive them another inch. We unyoked the oxen; we had about seventy pounds of flour; we took it out and divided it into four packs. Each of the men took about 18 pounds apiece and a blanket. I carried a little bacon, dried meat, and little quilt; I had in all about twelve pounds. We had one pint of flour a day for our alloyance. Sometimes we made soup of it; sometimes we (made) pancakes; and sometimes mixed it up with cold water and eat it that way. We traveld twelve or fourteen days. The time came at last when we should have to reach some place or starve. We saw fresh horse and cattle tracks. The morning come, we scraped all the flour out of the sack, mixed it up,

*and baked it into bread, and made some soup, and
eat everything we had. We traveld on all day
without anything to eat, and that evening we
Caught up with a sheep train of eight wagons.
We traveld with them till we arrived at the settle-
ments ; and know I am safe in California, and
got to good home, and going to school.*

*" Jerry is working in ——.   It is a good country.
You can get from 50 to 60.75 Dollars for cooking.
Tell me all about the affairs in the States, and how
all the folks get along."*

And so ends this artless narrative.   The little
man was at school again, God bless him ! while
his brother lay scalped upon the deserts.

FELLOW-PASSENGERS

A T Ogden we changed cars from the Union
Pacific to the Central Pacific line of railroad.
The change was doubly welcome ; for, first, we
had better cars on the new line ; and, second,
those in which we had been cooped for more
than ninety hours had begun to stink abomin-
ably. Several yards away, as we returned, let
us say from dinner, our nostrils were assailed
by rancid air. I have stood on a platform while
the whole train was shunting ; and as the dwelling-
cars drew near, there would come a whiff of pure
menagerie, only a little sourer, as from men
instead of monkeys. I think we are human only
in virtue of open windows. Without fresh air,
you only require a bad heart, and a remarkable
command of the Queen's English, to become
such another as Dean Swift ; a kind of leering,
human goat, leaping and wagging your scut on
mountains of offence. I do my best to keep my
head the other way, and look for the human
rather than the bestial in this Yahoo-like business
of the emigrant train. But one thing I must
say, the car of the Chinese was notably the
least offensive.

The cars on the Central Pacific were nearly
twice as high, and so proportionally airier ; they

were freshly varnished, which gave us all a sense
of cleanliness as though we had bathed; the
seats drew out and joined in the centre, so that
there was no more need for bed-boards; and
there was an upper tier of berths which could be
closed by day and opened at night.

I had by this time some opportunity of seeing
the people whom I was among. They were in
rather marked contrast to the emigrants I had
met on board ship while crossing the Atlantic.
They were mostly lumpish fellows, silent and
noisy, a common combination; somewhat sad,
I should say, with an extraordinary poor taste in
humour, and little interest in their fellow-
creatures beyond that of a cheap and merely
external curiosity. If they heard a man's name
and business, they seemed to think they had
the heart of that mystery; but they were as
eager to know that much as they were indifferent
to the rest. Some of them were on nettles till
they learned your name was Dickson and you a
journeyman baker; but beyond that, whether
you were Catholic or Mormon, dull or clever,
fierce or friendly, was all one to them. Others
who were not so stupid, gossiped a little, and, I
am bound to say, unkindly. A favourite witti-
cism was for some lout to raise the alarm of " All
aboard ! " while the rest of us were dining, thus
contributing his mite to the general discomfort.
Such a one was always much applauded for his
high spirits. When I was ill coming through
Wyoming, I was astonished—fresh from the

eager humanity on board ship—to meet with little but laughter. One of the young men even amused himself by incommoding me, as was then very easy ; and that not from ill-nature, but mere clod-like incapacity to think, for he expected me to join the laughter. I did so, but it was phantom merriment. Later on, a man from Kansas had three violent epileptic fits, and though, of course, there were not wanting some to help him, it was rather superstitious terror than sympathy that his case evoked among his fellow-passengers. " Oh, I hope he's not going to die ! " cried a woman ; " it would be terrible to have a dead body ! " And there was a very general movement to leave the man behind at the next station. This, by good fortune, the conductor negatived.

There was a good deal of story-telling in some quarters ; in others, little but silence. In this society, more than any other that ever I was in, it was the narrator alone who seemed to enjoy the narrative. It was rarely that any one listened for the listening. If he leant an ear to another man's story, it was because he was in immediate want of a hearer for one of his own. Food and the progress of the train were the subjects most generally treated ; many joined to discuss these who otherwise would hold their tongues. One small knot had no better occupation than to worm out of me my name ; and the more they tried, the more obstinately fixed I grew to baffle them. They assailed me with artful questions

and insidious offers of correspondence in the
future ; but I was perpetually on my guard,
and parried their assaults with inward laughter.
I am sure Dubuque would have given me ten
dollars for the secret. He owed me far more,
had he understood life, for thus preserving him a
lively interest throughout the journey. I met
one of my fellow-passengers months after, driving
a street tramway car in San Francisco ; and, as
the joke was now out of season, told him my name
without subterfuge. You never saw a man more
chop-fallen. But had my name been Demo-
gorgon, after so prolonged a mystery he had still
been disappointed.

There were no emigrants direct from Europe—
save one German family and a knot of Cornish
miners who kept grimly by themselves, one reading
the New Testament all day long through steel
spectacles, the rest discussing privately the
secrets of their old-world, mysterious race.
Lady Hester Stanhope believed she could make
something great of the Cornish ; for my part, I
can make nothing of them at all. A division of
races, older and more original than that of
Babel, keeps this close, esoteric family apart
from neighbouring Englishmen. Not even a
Red Indian seems more foreign in my eyes.
This is one of the lessons of travel—that some
of the strangest races dwell next door to you at
home.

The rest were all American born, but they
came from almost every quarter of that continent.

All the States of the North had sent out a
fugitive to cross the plains with me. From
Virginia, from Pennsylvania, from New York,
from far western Iowa and Kansas, from Maine
that borders on the Canadas, and from the
Canadas themselves—some one or two were
fleeing in quest of a better land and better
wages. The talk in the train, like the talk I
heard on the steamer, ran upon hard times,
short commons, and hope that moves ever
westward. I thought of my shipful from Great
Britain with a feeling of despair. They had come
3000 miles, and yet not far enough. Hard times
bowed them out of the Clyde, and stood to
welcome them at Sandy Hook. Where were
they to go ? Pennsylvania, Maine, Iowa, Kansas ?
These were not places for immigration, but for
emigration, it appeared ; not one of them, but
I knew a man who had lifted up his heel and left
it for an ungrateful country. And it was still
westward that they ran. Hunger, you would
have thought, came out of the east like the sun,
and the evening was made of edible gold. And,
meantime, in the car in front of me, were there
not half a hundred emigrants from the opposite
quarter ? Hungry Europe and hungry China,
each pouring from their gates in search of
provender, had here come face to face. The
two waves had met ; east and west had alike
failed ; the whole round world had been pro-
spected and condemned ; there was no El
Dorado anywhere ; and till one could emigrate

to the moon, it seemed as well to stay patiently
at home. Nor was there wanting another sign,
at once more picturesque and more dishearten-
ing ; for, as we continued to steam westward
toward the land of gold, we were continually
passing other emigrant trains upon the journey
east ; and these were as crowded as our own.
Had all these return voyagers made a fortune
in the mines ? Were they all bound for Paris,
and to be in Rome by Easter ? It would seem
not, for, whenever we met them, the passengers
ran on the platform and cried to us through the
windows, in a kind of wailing chorus, to " Come
back." On the plains of Nebraska, in the
mountains of Wyoming, it was still the same cry,
and dismal to my heart, " Come back ! " That
was what we heard by the way " about the good
country we were going to." And at that very
hour the Sand-lot of San Francisco was crowded
with the unemployed, and the echo from the
other side of Market Street was repeating the
rant of demagogues.

If, in truth, it were only for the sake of wages
that men emigrate, how many thousands would
regret the bargain ! But wages, indeed, are only
one consideration out of many ; for we are a
race of gipsies, and love change and travel for
themselves.

DESPISED RACES

OF all stupid ill-feelings, the sentiment of my fellow-Caucasians towards our companions in the Chinese car was the most stupid and the worst. They seemed never to have looked at them, listened to them, or thought of them, but hated them *a priori*. The Mongols were their enemies in that cruel and treacherous battle-field of money. They could work better and cheaper in half a hundred industries, and hence there was no calumny too idle for the Caucasians to repeat, and even to believe. They declared them hideous vermin, and affected a kind of choking in the throat when they beheld them. Now, as a matter of fact, the young Chinese man is so like a large class of European women, that on raising my head and suddenly catching sight of one at a considerable distance, I have for an instant been deceived by the resemblance. I do not say it is the most attractive class of our women, but for all that many a man's wife is less pleasantly favoured. Again, my emigrants declared that the Chinese were dirty. I cannot say they were clean, for that was impossible upon the journey ; but in their efforts after cleanliness they put the rest of us to shame. We all pigged and stewed in one

infamy, wet our hands and faces for half a
minute daily on the platform, and were un-
ashamed. But the Chinese never lost an opportunity, and you would see them washing their
feet—an act not dreamed of among ourselves—
and going as far as decency permitted to wash
their whole bodies. I may remark by the way
that the dirtier people are in their persons the
more delicate is their sense of modesty. A clean
man strips in a crowded boathouse ; but he who
is unwashed slinks in and out of bed without
uncovering an inch of skin. Lastly, these very
foul and malodorous Caucasians entertained the
surprising illusion that it was the Chinese waggon,
and that alone, which stank. I have said
already that it was the exception, and notably
the freshest of the three.

These judgments are typical of the feeling in
all Western America. The Chinese are considered stupid, because they are imperfectly
acquainted with English. They are held to be
base because their dexterity and frugality enable
them to underbid the lazy, luxurious Caucasian.
They are said to be thieves ; I am sure they have
no monopoly of that. They are called cruel ; the
Anglo-Saxon and the cheerful Irishman may
each reflect before he bears the accusation. I am
told, again, that they are of the race of river
pirates, and belong to the most despised and
dangerous class in the Celestial Empire. But if
this be so, what remarkable pirates have we
here ! and what must be the virtues, the in-

dustry, the education, and the intelligence of
their superiors at home !

A while ago it was the Irish, now it is the
Chinese that must go. Such is the cry. It
seems, after all, that no country is bound to
submit to immigration any more than to invasion :
each is war to the knife, and resistance to either
but legitimate defence. Yet we may regret the
free tradition of the republic, which loved to
depict herself with open arms, welcoming all
unfortunates. And certainly, as a man who
believes that he loves freedom, I may be excused
some bitterness when I find her sacred name
misused in the contention. It was but the other
day that I heard a vulgar fellow in the Sand-lot,
the popular tribune of San Francisco, roaring for
arms and butchery. " At the call of Abreham
Lincoln," said the orator, " ye rose in the name
of freedom to set free the negroes ; can ye not
rise and liberate yourselves from a few dhirty
Mongolians ? "

For my own part, I could not look but with
wonder and respect on the Chinese. Their forefathers watched the stars before mine had begun
to keep pigs. Gunpowder and printing, which
the other day we imitated, and a school of
manners which we never had the delicacy so
much as to desire to imitate, were theirs in a
long-past antiquity. They walk the earth with
us, but it seems they must be of different clay.
They hear the clock strike the same hour, yet
surely of a different epoch. They travel by

steam conveyance, yet with such a baggage of
old Asiatic thoughts and superstitions as might
check the locomotive in its course. Whatever
is thought within the circuit of the Great Wall;
what the wry-eyed, spectacled schoolmaster
teaches in the hamlets round Pekin; religions so
old that our language looks a halfling boy alongside; philosophy so wise that our best philo-
sophers find things therein to wonder at; all
this travelled alongside of me for thousands of
miles over plain and mountain. Heaven knows
if we had one common thought or fancy all that
way, or whether our eyes, which yet were formed
upon the same design, beheld the same world
out of the railway windows. And when either
of us turned his thoughts to home and childhood,
what a strange dissimilarity must there not have
been in these pictures of the mind—when I
beheld that old, grey, castled city, high throned
above the firth, with the flag of Britain flying,
and the red-coat sentry pacing over all; and the
man in the next car to me would conjure up some
junks and a pagoda and a fort of porcelain, and
call it, with the same affection, home.

Another race shared among my fellow-passengers in disfavour of the Chinese; and that, it
is hardly necessary to say, was the noble red man
of old story—he over whose own hereditary
continent we had been steaming all these days.
I saw no wild or independent Indian; indeed, I
hear that such avoid the neighbourhood of the
train; but now and again at way-stations, a

husband and wife and a few children, disgracefully dressed out with the sweepings of civilisation, came forth and stared upon the emigrants. The silent stoicism of their conduct, and the pathetic degradation of their appearance, would have touched any thinking creature, but my fellow-passengers danced and jested round them with a truly Cockney baseness. I was ashamed for the thing we call civilisation. We should carry upon our consciences so much at least, of our forefathers' misconduct as we continue to profit by ourselves.

If oppression drives a wise man mad, what should be raging in the hearts of these poor tribes, who have been driven back and back, step after step, their promised reservations torn from them one after another as the States extended westward, until at length they are shut up into these hideous mountain deserts of the centre—and even there find themselves invaded, insulted, and hunted out by ruffianly diggers? The eviction of the Cherokees (to name but an instance), the extortion of Indian agents, the outrages of the wicked, the ill-faith of all, nay, down to the ridicule of such poor beings as were here with me upon the train, make up a chapter of injustice and indignity such as a man must be in some ways base if his heart will suffer him to pardon or forget. These old, well-founded, historical hatreds have a savour of nobility for the independent. That the Jew should not love the Christian, nor the Irishman

love the English, nor the Indian brave tolerate
the thought of the American, is not disgraceful
to the nature of man ; rather, indeed, honourable,
since it depends on wrongs ancient like the race,
and not personal to him who cherishes the indignation.

TO THE GOLDEN GATES

A LITTLE corner of Utah is soon traversed, and leaves no particular impressions on the mind. By an early hour on Wednesday morning we stopped to breakfast at Toano, a little station on a bleak, high-lying plateau in Nevada. The man who kept the station eating-house was a Scot, and learning that I was the same, he grew very friendly, and gave me some advice on the country I was now entering. "You see," said he, " I tell you this, because I come from your country." Hail, brither Scots !

His most important hint was on the moneys of this part of the world. There is something in the simplicity of a decimal coinage which is revolting to the human mind ; thus the French, in small affairs, reckon strictly by half-pence ; and you have to solve, by a spasm of mental arithmetic, such posers as thirty-two, forty-five, or even a hundred halfpence. In the Pacific States they have made a bolder push for complexity, and settle their affairs by a coin that no longer exists— the *bit*, or old Mexican real. The supposed value of the bit is twelve and a halfcents, eight to the dollar. When it comes to two bits, the quarter-dollar stands for the required amount. But how about an odd bit ? The nearest coin to it is a

dime, which is short by a fifth. That, then, is
called a *short bit*. If you have one, you lay it
triumphantly down, and save two and a half
cents. But if you have not, and lay down a
quarter, the bar-keeper or shopman calmly
tenders you a dime by way of change ; and thus
you have paid what is called a *long bit*, and lost
two and a half cents, or even, by comparison
with a short bit, five cents. In country places
all over the Pacific coast, nothing lower than a
bit is ever asked or taken, which vastly increases
the cost of life ; as even for a glass of beer you
must pay fivepence or sevenpence-halfpenny, as
the case may be. You would say that this
system of mutual robbery was as broad as it was
long ; but I have discovered a plan to make it
broader, with which I here endow the public.
It is brief and simple—radiantly simple. There
is one place where five cents are recognised, and
that is the post-office. A quarter is only worth
two bits, a short and a long. Whenever you
have a quarter, go to the post-office and buy
five cents worth of postage-stamps ; you will
receive in change two dimes, that is,. two short
bits. The purchasing power of your money is
undiminished. You can go and have your two
glasses of beer all the same ; and you have made
yourself a present of five cents' worth of postage-
stamps into the bargain. Benjamin Franklin
would have patted me on the head for this
discovery.

From Toano we travelled all day through

deserts of alkali and sand, horrible to man, and bare sage-brush country that seemed little kindlier, and came by supper-time to Elko. As we were standing, after our manner, outside the station, I saw two men whip suddenly from underneath the cars, and take to their heels across country. They were tramps, it appeared, who had been riding on the beams since eleven of the night before; and several of my fellow-passengers had already seen and conversed with them while we broke our fast at Toano. These land stowaways play a great part over here in America, and I should have liked dearly to become acquainted with them.

At Elko an odd circumstance befell me. I was coming out from supper, when I was stopped by a small, stout, ruddy man, followed by two others taller and ruddier than himself.

" Ex-cuse me, sir," he said, " but do you happen to be going on ? "

I said I was, whereupon he said he hoped to dissuade me to desist from that intention. He had a situation to offer me, and if we could come to terms, why, good and well. " You see," he continued, " I'm running a theatre here, and we're a little short in the orchestra. You're a musician, I guess ? "

I assured him that, beyond a rudimentary acquaintance with " Auld Lang Syne " and " The Wearing of the Green," I had no pretension whatever to that style. He seemed much put out of countenance; and one of his taller

companions asked him, on the nail, for five
dollars.

" You see, sir," added the latter to me, " he
bet you were a musician ; I bet you weren't.
No offence, I hope ? "

" None whatever," I said, and the two with-
drew to the bar, where I presume the debt was
liquidated.

This little adventure woke bright hopes in my
fellow-travellers, who thought they had now
come to a country where situations went a-
begging. But I am not so sure that the offer
was in good faith. Indeed, I am more than
half persuaded it was but a feeler to decide the
bet.

Of all the next day I will tell you nothing, for
the best of all reasons, that I remember no more
than that we continued through desolate and
desert scenes, fiery hot and deadly weary. But
some time after I had fallen asleep that night,
I was awakened by one of my companions. It
was in vain that I resisted. A fire of enthusiasm
and whisky burned in his eyes ; and he declared
we were in a new country, and I must come forth
upon the platform and see with my own eyes.
The train was then, in its patient way, standing
halted in a by-track. It was a clear, moonlit
night ; but the valley was too narrow to admit
the moonshine direct, and only a diffused glimmer
whitened the tall rocks and relieved the blackness of the pines. A hoarse clamour filled the
air ; it was the continuous plunge of a cascade

somewhere near at hand among the mountains. The air struck chill, but tasted good and vigorous in the nostrils—a fine, dry, old mountain atmosphere. I was dead sleepy, but I returned to roost with a grateful mountain feeling at my heart.

When I awoke next morning, I was puzzled for a while to know if it were day or night, for the illumination was unusual. I sat up at last, and found we were grading slowly downward through a long snowshed; and suddenly we shot into an open; and before we were swallowed into the next length of wooden tunnel, I had one glimpse of a huge pine-forested ravine upon my left, a foaming river, and a sky already coloured with the fires of dawn. I am usually very calm over the displays of nature; but you will scarce believe how my heart leaped at this. It was like meeting one's wife. I had come home again— home from unsightly deserts to the green and habitable corners of the earth. Every spire of pine along the hill-top, every trouty pool along that mountain river, was more dear to me than a blood relation. Few people have praised God more happily than I did. And thenceforward, down by Blue Cañon, Alta, Dutch Flat, and all the old mining camps, through a sea of mountain forests, dropping thousands of feet toward the far sea-level as we went, not I only, but all the passengers on board, threw off their sense of dirt and heat and weariness, and bawled like schoolboys, and thronged with shining eyes

upon the platform and became new creatures
within and without.   The sun no longer oppressed
us with heat, it only shone laughingly along the
mountain-side, until we were fain to laugh ourselves for glee.   At every turn we could see
farther into the land and our own happy futures.
At every town the cocks were tossing their clear
notes into the golden air, and crowing for the
new day and the new country.   For this was
indeed our destination ;   this was " the good
country " we had been going to so long.

By afternoon we were at Sacramento, the city
of gardens in a plain of corn ; and the next day
before the dawn we were lying-to upon the
Oakland side of San Francisco Bay.   The day
was breaking as we crossed the ferry ; the fog
was rising over the citied hills of San Francisco ;
the bay was perfect—not a ripple, scarce a stain,
upon its blue expanse ; everything was waiting,
breathless, for the sun.   A spot of cloudy gold
lit first upon the head of Tamalpais, and then
widened downward on its shapely shoulder ; the
air seemed to awaken, and began to sparkle ;
and suddenly

"The tall hills Titan discovered,"

and the city of San Francisco, and the bay of
gold and corn, were lit from end to end with
summer daylight.